BORN OF THE SPIRIT

BORN
OF THE
SPIRIT

Renewal Movements
In the Life of the Church

Bishop Paul J. Cordes

GREENLAWN PRESS

ISBN 0-937779-30-X

Library of Congress Card Catalog Number 94-79332.

Originally published in German under the title *Den Geist nicht auslöschen: Charismen und Neuevangelisierung*, copyright © Verlag Herder, Freiburg im Breisgau 1990. © 1991. English translation © 1992 St. Paul's, Slough, United Kingdom. First published in the United Kingdom by St. Paul's, Slough, under the title *Charisms and New Evangelization* (ISBN 0-85439-403-6).

This edition, slightly edited for American readers, is published by Greenlawn Press, 107 S. Greenlawn, South Bend, IN 46617.

00 99 98 97 96 95 5 4 3 2 1

Printed in the United States of America.

Contents

But whatever be the risk of corruption from intercourse with the world around, such a risk must be encountered if a great idea is duly to be understood, and much more if it is to be fully exhibited. It is elicited and expanded by trial, and battles into perfection and supremacy. Nor does it escape the collision of opinion even in its earlier days, nor does it remain truer to itself, and with a better claim to be considered one and the same, though externally protected from vicissitudes and change. . . . It changes (with the world around it) in order to remain the same. In a higher world it is otherwise, but here below to live is to change, and to be perfect is to have changed often.

Cardinal John Henry Newman (1845)
"On the Development of Christian Doctrine"

What sounds full of hope throughout the universal church—and this even in the midst of the crisis that the church is going through in the Western world—is the upsurge of new movements that no one has planned and no one called into being, but that simply emerge of their own accord from the inner vitality of the faith. What is becoming apparent in them—albeit very faintly—is something very similar to a pentecostal hour in the church. I am thinking for instance of the Charismatic Renewal movement, the Neocatechumenate, the *Cursillo* movement, the *Focolarini*, Communion and Liberation and so on. All these movements undoubtedly raise many problems, but this is invariably the case in everything that is truly alive.

Cardinal Joseph Ratzinger (1985)

FOREWORD

"New evangelization": the expression has undoubtedly enjoyed a certain vogue in our time. Any statistical survey of current buzz words would probably assign it a leading place among the most used phrases in the church today. As enunciated by the church's pastors, administrators and planners, the expression is to be understood in the first place as an appeal. It intends, in other words, to urge us all to carry out the missionary commandment of Jesus Christ: "Go into the whole world and proclaim the gospel to every creature" (Mk. 16:15). New evangelization is therefore the enunciation of a goal for the future. Yet occasionally it is also possible to discover that the Lord of the church is already, here and now, practicing this new evangelization. He has given charisms to men and women who are proclaiming the Good News loudly and clearly, in this way witnessing its power to human beings and thus challenging them to a fresh listening to the word of God.

The church's hierarchy and co-workers are especially faced by the task of giving scope to these charisms, once they have been recognized as genuine. The Second Vatican Council had already urged the representatives of the priestly ministry to "discover with faith, recognize with joy, and foster with diligence the many and varied charismatic gifts of the laity, whether these be of a humble or more exalted kind" (*Decree on the Ministry and Life of Priests, Presbyterorum Ordinis*, no. 9). Yet the duty of fostering these charisms urged by the council does not seem to be easy to fulfill. Already at the biblical level the Apostle of the Gentiles felt obliged to admonish his community: "Do not quench the Spirit. Do not despise prophecies" (1 Th. 5:19-20). Evidently the ecclesial community has difficulty in allowing new expressions or movements of the Spirit, however well tested and approved, to operate freely.

New evangelization, then, as a litmus test of the Christian life? Spiritual movements are not appreciated in the way that the statistical recurrence of the expression would suggest. On the contrary, their impulses are greeted with skepticism; they

1

come into friction with the traditional structures; they frequently fail to clear the hurdles of the postconciliar consultative bodies; they are often passed over in silence by the church's media; they are regarded as playgrounds for outsiders.

"Do not quench the Spirit!" St. Paul does not demand anything that the community of the faithful did not in any case vouchsafe. This is also shown by a glance at the history of the church. It enables us to see that God continuously arouses charisms for the renewal of his church. It also confirms that these charisms, once awakened, not infrequently run the risk of being diluted or extinguished altogether.

The lessons of the past make it clear that, in the case of new evangelization, proper counsel and pastoral programs are certainly needed to ensure that God's liberating message should be resubmitted to the faithful. Yet even more striking is the lesson of history which shows how God's salvific initiative is often hindered by human blindness. This is borne out by the life and work of some great renewers: Anthony, the father of the desert; Athanasius, the theologian; Benedict, the founder of the Benedictine order; Francis and Ignatius. All these and many others have a warning for us: it was only after their deaths that they were accorded the "honors of the altar"; during their lifetimes they ran up against the most obstinate resistance at every level of the ecclesiastical hierarchy.

Yet, it may be asked, is the lesson of history trustworthy, especially if it is based on only a few examples? Is objectivity not lost in the process? Of course, it is beyond the scope of the brief investigation that follows to gather and present all the available data by the rigorous methods of historical inquiry. Rather, my purpose is simply to elucidate—on the basis of ascertained facts—a few more significant *tranches de vie*. The historian who trusts the true nature of the discipline he professes conceives of his investigation as being "committed." He knows that he himself is inevitably marked by the very history he is studying. He cannot place himself outside the event he is trying to understand and describe. In the last analysis he has no point of view outside the world. "History is what each of us was and is. It is the bond of our destiny." Understanding history thus means grasping "what has been given to us in history as something that appeals to us and calls out to us" (Hans Georg Gadamer).

INTRODUCTION

"The beloved of God is the church, so long as she walks in the footsteps of the Fathers. But now she has become Babylon through her hideousness and her inhabitation by unclean spirits, and for God himself an abomination. For who would not be beside himself with horror to see the church with an ass's head or the believing soul with wolf's teeth, a pig's snout, cheeks pale with terror, a bull's neck, and in everything else such a wildness and monstrousness that anyone seeing it is stricken dumb by terror? Who would not like to call and describe so tremendous a deformation as Babylon rather than the church of Christ? Who would not call it a wilderness rather than the City of God? . . . Because of this dreadful abomination of reprobates and lechers, who submerge the church in such great numbers that the others remain hidden and invisible among all the chaff, the heretics call the church a whore and Babylon, and, if we look at the reprobates and the Christians merely in name, they might justifiably feel and speak in this way, but not extend these opprobrious epithets to Christians as a whole. A bride she is no longer, but a monster of terrible deformity and savageness . . . , and it is clear that, in such a condition, it will not be said of her: "Thou art all fair; there is no spot in thee.'"[1]

So wrote William of Auvergne, bishop of Paris, in the 13th century, in his commentary on the Song of Songs.

The church is indeed not just the "community of saints" we proclaim in our Creed. She is no less justifiably considered a gathering of sinners. Ever since her foundation she has suffered confusion and godlessness; she has been threatened by division and evil.

The Apostles themselves earned the rebuke of the Lord by quarreling among themselves about the places they should occupy at the side of Christ sitting in glory (Mk. 10:35-45). The original community of the faithful was itself punished by the severe sentence handed out by God on Ananias and Sapphira, when they went behind Peter's back and tried to enrich themselves (Ac. 5:1 ff.). The Apostle of the Gentiles himself had to

3

struggle for the essential nucleus of the gospel of salvation, which he saw jeopardized among the Galatians (Gal. 3:1).

Anyone who wants to write the history of the church as a scandal sheet will certainly find no shortage of suitable material in every period. It is only in the present time that her image, at least in the experience of many contemporaries, is improving. At any rate, most church people seem to think that their own house is not in such bad shape. In their "situation reports" they underline the altruistic commitment of those who no longer consider themselves Christians, and point encouragingly to the growing number of people of good will. It would be better, they imply, if terms such as "unbeliever" or "nonpracticing Christian" were to be eliminated from our pastoral vocabulary, since they could have a detrimental effect.

Instead of lamenting over the decline of faith, it would be better to consider the altruistic dedication of those who put the gospel injunction of love for their fellow men into practice, without identifying themselves with the church. Is it not in them that God's love is made manifest?

While the statistics about participation in the life of the church are not exactly rosy,[2] those who are worried about the fate of the church run the risk of appearing as Jeremiahs or even outright pessimists. Anyone who devotes himself with new-won strength to the proclamation of the gospel and the deepening of the faith arouses embarrassment or encounters incomprehension. If he comes armed with new ideas or pastoral initiatives, he is seen as disturbing the tranquillity of the local church and the harmony of its various postconciliar consultative bodies.

In the specific circumstances of everyday life, such animosities only help to foster misunderstandings. The innovator is observed with scrupulous attention. As soon as he makes a false step or commits an error, the fact is speedily generalized. Of course, no one objects in principle to the attempt to take the gospel seriously. Yet, if someone should set himself this goal, he ought—the feeling goes—to proceed with all due discretion without irritating others or generating tensions by criticizing the status quo.

Should such a preservation of harmony at all costs become normative in our time? Is the course that we in the church are steering so reliable that even the attempt to examine it is considered as unnecessarily rocking the boat, and that of actually criticizing it even worse? Hans Urs von Balthasar, whose knowledge of the spiritual currents in our time was surely unparalleled, has bequeathed us an analysis that brands as mendacity any reconciliation made merely for the preservation of peace.[3] He identifies in the church of our time a trend toward the supersession—indeed, even the erosion—of faith by factual knowledge. Christian thought, in his view, suffers from a split that reaches down to its very foundations. Hitherto the articles of faith were regarded as no longer questionable objects of Christian theological inquiry; today, by contrast, this understanding has been reversed. Precisely these articles—both their content and the act of faith they demand—are subjected to rational investigation and most of them end up by assuming a new content, one that is essentially reduced to the level of anthropological plausibility. Rationalism has penetrated into Catholic theology, for the conviction has grown that it is only by its help that the faith can be made comprehensible for nonbelievers.

The theologian of Lucerne then recalls the instructions which spiritual literature offers for the battle of the spirit and for the necessary discernment of spirits. Without this discernment the battle cannot be fought, for the duel is a superhuman one. "It consists not just of a purely human battle about words or ideas, but of involvement in the great theo-dramatic battle that has erupted between God and his Logos on the one hand and the infernal Anti-Logos on the other. Therefore he who takes part in it must grasp 'the sword of the Spirit, i.e., the Word of God'; this means not leading a rearguard action, but facing the adversary eye to eye" (*op. cit.*, 432).

New ferment in the church, and appeals to an examination of conscience, will therefore encounter opposition. The message of renewal mainly irritates fellow Christians and is accepted by only a small proportion of them. Yet it has always happened in the church that the "small flock" has had to drag along with them a large number of those whose faith, hope and love have been enfeebled. Augustine found an allusion to this fact in Psalm 48:10: "O God, we ponder your kindness within your temple." In one of his sermons the bishop of Hippo in fact points out that those who have attained mercy clearly cannot be compared with those in whose midst God's mercy is attained. He declares: "In the midst of your people, who find no mercy, we receive your mercy. For 'he came unto his own, and his own received him not.'" Many who receive the sacraments have kept the appearance of piety, although they have not lived in conformity with the grace of baptism.[4]

Whoever is urged by fidelity to the church to proclaim the Lord should not therefore be too promptly placed among the typical prophets of doom and reduced to silence; inveterate pessimists do not appeal for conversion and reform. The church herself prays during Holy Week each year: "Be converted, be converted to the Lord your God!" She has every reason for repeating this prayer, and Hans Urs von Balthasar finds himself in the best company, together with Augustine and William of Auvergne.

Each of these three men spoke for his time. They confronted us with the history of the church. Fortunately, that history does not begin just in our century. The past can therefore provide help and guidance to us. Events of earlier periods may reveal to us contents and methods that may help us to restore Christian authenticity.

A careful examination of attempts made to renew the church will discover in them many points of similarity. We find in the past certain individuals who answered the call to conversion, and thus accepted a closer bond with God. Some of their contemporaries were impressed and won over by their example. Groups came to be formed round the initiators. Communities of initiates, religious orders, or even sects, thus developed. The parallels detectable among these various developments have had the consequence of exciting the interest of sociology in the phenomenon.[5] Nor can fundamental theological reflection fail to overlook the fact that Jesus Christ's words and deeds themselves can be interpreted in a similar way. Can he not be seen as someone who came to renew the Old Testament, and to establish a new and deeper rooting of the Jewish people in the will of God?[6]

NOTES

1. Cited in: H.U. von Balthasar, "*Casta Meretrix*," in: *ibid.*, *Sponsa Verbi. Skizzen zur Theologie*, II, Einsiedeln 1960, 203-205, here 207.

2. See H. Maier, "*Vergegenwärtigung des Glaubens*," in: *Die Zukunft des Glaubens*, ed. by the Secretariat of the German Bishops' Conference

and the General Secretariat of the Central Committee of German Catholics, Bonn 1989, 7-21, here 7 ff.

3. See H.U. von Balthasar, *Theodramatik*, III, Einsiedeln 1980, 423-38.

4. In: *Die Feier des Stundengebets, Lektionar*, I, Jahresreihe 7, Freiburg 1979, 205 ff.

5. See J. Wach, *Religionssoziologie*, Tübingen 1951, 147-231; W. Stark, *The Sociology of Religion: A Study of Christendom*, vols. I-V, here vol. III, London and New York 1967, 249-440. The sociologist of religion Werner Stark has clearly not so far received his due, nor has the significance of his work been adequately recognized in Europe. However, in the course of an obituary notice, "In memoriam Werner Stark" (*Kölner Zeitschrift für Soziologie und Sozialpsychologie*, 38, 1986, 197 ff.), J. Stagl underlines his great importance, pointing out that he had the courage and the strength to pose radical questions and to embark on a major synthesis. "Both Stark's *magna opera*," writes Stagl, "still await their discovery . . . but their bibliographical details are formidable in their range."

6. J. Ratzinger, "*Was heisst Erneuerung in der Kirche?*," in: *ibid.*, *Das neue Volk Gottes*, Dusseldorf 1969, 267-281, here 275 ff.

I. "Go forth from the land"
Genesis 12:1

We know very well that the cultural and spiritual roots of Jesus of Nazareth, like those of every member of the Chosen People, lie clearly in the Old Testament and in Jewish religious life. About his hidden life, though, we know only a few significant details. It is only with his first appearance in public, and the inception of his public ministry, that the image we have of his person is enriched with detail and acquires a clearly defined profile.

The same is true of most of those who, following in his footsteps, have called for conversion. Their initiative only becomes significant once they begin speaking out in their own community of origin. From that moment onward public attention is drawn to them. Concepts of faith and pastoral plans are formulated in response to them. Both the past and future of the community arouse interest, for the new must be justified by comparison with the old.

The convictions that distinguish the new beginning derive from the subsoil from which they grew. For no one can deny his ancestry or repudiate his origin. Both will accompany him in one way or another, even if it is only with the function of negative delimitation or of arousing protest. In spite of this, it is the new beginning that characterizes reform and those that espouse it; it is the idea and its orientation that distinguish it from the soil from which it sprang. By a deliberate "turnabout," a new direction is chosen.

This "turnabout" almost always finds expression in practical action. The groups or their founders seek a new social environment. They deliberately change their place of residence. They do so in the same way that the Lord himself sought exile in the Decapolis—the pagan territory of the ten cities—in order to instruct his disciples more intensively, and progressively detach them from the synagogue.[1] The Lord chose a different place of residence not only for fear of persecutions, but also to wean his followers from the sphere of influence by which they had largely been characterized in the past.

The "method" of emigration points to a first significant criterion of reform and renewal. It is one that can be seen, even more clearly than in Jesus, in the Egyptian monks who sought refuge in the wilderness. The most famous of these desert fathers was St. Anthony (d. 356).

1. Solitude in the desert

Anthony was the son of well-to-do Christian parents in central Egypt. We know this from Athanasius, who wrote his life and also made him known to the church in the West. Egypt in the third century was on the whole economically prosperous. Its inhabitants were distinguished by a heightened consciousness of their own worth. They were convinced they occupied a special place in God's plan of salvation. Had not Mary, Joseph and the infant Jesus sought refuge in their country, on being persecuted by Herod? Had not the Israelites in the wilderness reproached God for leading them away from "the fleshpots of Egypt," where they had eaten bread to the full? In Anthony's time, it was Egypt, not Canaan, that was the real promised land for Christians.

Anyone living in the heart of Europe, and ignorant of the historical circumstances, who presumes that the so-called desert fathers were already living in a desert-like land before their exodus, would be mistaken: the journey into solitude, the path into the wilderness, started out from one of the proudest and most nourishing places in the world of that time. It is not by chance that Alexandria was called the "new Athens," and considered the second most important city in the world. Luxury and affluence flourished in it. It thronged with merchants and traders, who offered their luxury consumer goods—fine leather, exquisite ivory mirrors and glassware—to the peoples of the Mediterranean basin.[2]

In his biography of St. Anthony, Henri Queffélec has described more fully the circumstances from which he sprang, and which made him repudiate so passionately the Christian life-style of his contemporaries. To begin with, during the persecution of the Emperor Decius (d. 251), it is clear that many members of the church in Egypt had not exactly conducted themselves in a heroic way (pp. 18 ff., 132). Subsequently, men like Bishop Nepos of Arsinoe were expecting a millennial earthly kingdom of the Messiah, in which to experience the joys of the world, according to a form of speculation typical of people used to prosperity, and that erroneously sought justification in the book of Revelation. Anthony, a man permeated and fired by faith, evidently saw no other alternative but that of a radical break with the past: a completely fresh start. Queffélec writes: " . . . in this third century Christianity could still appear as a movement of revolutionary rabble-rousers. Yet in the depths of their hearts these men—i.e., men like Anthony—had realized that it was becoming too middle-class and matter-of-fact; that it was adorning itself with Greek tinsel; that it was becoming infected with heathen ideas and turning political. And each of them (it is significant that we are dealing with a whole category, and that no one gave the first signal) had chosen to withdraw from these currents, separating himself from the Christian-heathens and the heathen-Christians and retreating into solitude to cultivate his asceticism. Even so, the discoveries they made would one day become common property, and in the end their service to Christianity was to be far greater than that of Emperor Constantine himself, with all his legions and all his cleverness" (*op. cit.*, 75 ff.).

Yet this exodus did not occur without any involvement in the fate of the local church and its members. When the Emperor Diocletian (d. 305) ordered his bloody persecution, Anthony in fact returned from the wilderness to the epicenter of events (pp. 161 ff., 168 ff.). We encounter him in Alexandria for some time, but once the storm had passed he returned to the desert. He needed to distance himself geographically, so that his fresh start, his attempted renewal, might gain in spiritual depth. He used the new and very different conditions of life in the desert to recover the forgotten contents of Christian life and give them greater clarity.

Men of the following generations confirmed this. In the documents they left us, it becomes abundantly clear that the change of place and the new conditions of life in the desert actually did permit a deepening of the faith; indeed, that the circumstances of Christendom in effect left no other choice to those who were true to their faith. "After the death of the Apostle, the mass of the faithful began to cool in their ardor. . . . But there were men in whom the fire of the apostolic age still

11

glowed. In order to remain faithful to the original model [of the faith], they abandoned the cities and the society of those who believed that they themselves and the church could settle into a comfortable life without any asceticism. Some of them therefore retreated into the environs of the cities and into solitude. They began by themselves to observe the rules which, as they well knew, the Apostles had laid down for the entire body of the church. . . . They sought solitude neither out of fear nor out of an unhealthy excess of zeal, but because they yearned for a higher perfection and a contemplative dedication to God. . . . With good reason, therefore, are they called 'anchorites,' or 'men of the exodus.' "[3]

Anthony and the monks opened the eyes of whole generations of the faithful to the struggle against "the principalities and powers" (Ep. 6:12), against whom they had already been put on their guard by the Apostle Paul. The hundreds of stories that the church has bequeathed us about them are inestimable nourishment for growth in the Spirit.

The close and intimate bond with God that distinguished the desert fathers also prepared the spiritual ground in the church for the theological assault on the heresy of Arianism, which repudiated one of the central truths of the faith, the doctrine of the divinity of Christ. Without the school of the desert, would not St. Athanasius (d. 373), the disciple and biographer of Anthony, have been broken by the relentless persecution by his theological adversaries? As it was, he resisted five exiles for a total banishment of seventeen and a half years. He opposed the rationalistic dissolution of the mystery of the God who became Man, since he had learnt in obedient self-renunciation to discern whether the spirits come from God (1 Jn. 4:1). A man who has been tempered in solitude, and has fought the battle of the spirit, will not be seduced by deceitful appearances; he does not simply conform, does not compliantly accommodate himself. His retreat from day-to-day life gives him the strength to resist. The men who gathered round Athanasius constituted a phalanx against apostasy. In them the desert had liberated the spirit that preserved, within the church, faith in the co-essential divinity of the Son of God.[4]

2. The seclusion of the cloister

Renewal is not achieved without delimitation, without the definition of frontiers. Only by this means is it possible to be different. If the conscience of everyone is conformistically leveled, it is impossible to find the firm and undeviating point that alone can initiate change. Movements originate only if they have a different level than that of their surrounding environment.

What Anthony began by his retreat into the desert was aspired to two centuries later by St. Benedict (d. 547), by his seeking refuge in the mountain fastnesses, in the wild places of Italy, and then by the building of monasteries. After studying the liberal arts in Rome, he soon fled the loose morals of his university colleagues. The life of a hermit at Subiaco (in the Sabine Mountains), the formation of a circle of disciples at Aniotale and, eventually, the foundation of a monastery on Monte Cassino: these were the stages of a life that took Benedict into the wilderness.

Benedict in no way set himself the aim of exerting any influence on the church or society. He did not see himself as fulfilling any pastoral, much less social, function. Rather, he aspired with his community to the praise of God. Yet his monastic foundations were so fruitful that it is impossible, at least for present purposes, to attempt even a summary of them.[5] What more particularly interests us here above all is Benedict's new beginning, which took the form of an existential, and not verbal or demonstrational, protest. The preeminent meaning of the walls of the cloister and exile from society is that they enable the monks to develop a closer bond with God. This, for instance, is how Basil the Great (d. 379) expresses the matter: "Especially to be able to dedicate oneself to prayer it is necessary to retreat into solitude . . . we thus break with our old habits. . . . It is difficult, if not impossible, to leave everything as it was in life and yet at the same time to change or improve oneself."[6]

This is why the *Rule* of St. Benedict explicitly prescribes that, once it has been chosen, the cloister may not be abandoned (58, 15), nor may it be misunderstood as a dormitory for a life "in the midst of the world." In another passage the *Rule* goes so far as to prescribe as follows: "If possible, the monastery should be laid out in such a way that everything necessary, namely, water, mill and gardens, lies within its walls . . . and the various callings can be exercised within the monastery. The monks therefore have no need to roam around outside, as this is in no way salutary for their souls" (66, 6-7).

That the renewal of the Christian world was necessary is beyond doubt. It is enough to learn from St. Jerome (d. 419) about the abuses and misdemeanors of the clergy in his time to form an idea of the decadence and impotence of Christianity. This is what the combative Father of the church wrote to the young noblewoman Eustochium about his contemporaries: "There are others—and here I am speaking of men of my own class—who aspire to the office of presbyter or deacon just for the purpose of seeing women with greater freedom. As a consequence their one concern is about their dress, that it may be finely perfumed, and that their foot may not puff out because of a loose shoe. They roll their hair into ringlets with the aid of curling tongs, their fingers sparkle with rings. If they go into the street when it's wet, they walk mincingly, scarcely touching the ground, so as not to spatter their feet with mud. When one sees them, one would take them for suitors rather than priests. For some of these men the whole business of their life consists in discovering the names of married women and finding out about their homes and characters."[7]

This corrupt Christianity was reacted against by the cloistered hermits, who opposed it by their manifest dedication to God. Their existence and above all their life-style were in themselves a permanent challenge. A starker antithesis than that between the worldly priests of whom Jerome speaks and the Benedictine monks would be hard to imagine. The latter, even in winter, got up at two o'clock in the morning to sing Lauds; they had no personal possessions and their meals were frugal; they worked hard and, when their end came, they were laid to rest in the earth without any coffin. All this was true both of monks who came from poor families and those from wealthy backgrounds.

3. "Free from the bonds of all earthly desires"

The members of the monastic community fixed their gaze on God and ignored the effect that their dedication to the faith might have on the church and society at large. Conversely, their alternate form of life, hidden as they were behind the walls of the cloister, was little known to their Christian contemporaries. Occasionally those living nearby were in some way involved. The church hierarchy, too, was certainly aware of the cenobitic life of the monks. Yet it has to be said that in general their praise of God and ascetic life-style were not held up as a model to the people of God; for those engaged in the pursuit of the church's everyday life they remained hidden from view.

The appearance of the mendicant friars several centuries later brought a significant change to this situation. With the mendicants, monasticism was no longer practiced in a reserved sphere, in a state of self-seclusion. Since they lived on alms, they naturally gravitated toward human settlements and roamed through cities and towns. In this way they came into constant contact with all sections of the population. Their lifestyle and piety could thus radiate out to other Christians. The opportunities for apostolic witness increased. Admittedly the throng of renewers was small in the beginning, and their forces of transformation appeared weak, but they were fortified by the parable of our Lord that only a small amount of yeast is needed to leaven the whole mass of dough (Mt. 13:33).

What matters is that the dough is made substantially different in this way. Flour cannot transform itself into something different; yeast is needed. So, once again, it is exodus that produces the potential for transformation. This is a law that we find first and foremost in the life of St. Francis himself. He abandoned the environment to which he was accustomed. This is how St. Bonaventure describes the period early in 1206 in which Francis said goodbye to his father and to Assisi: "Now that he was free from the bonds of all earthly desires in his disregard for the world, Francis left the town and sought out a place where he could be alone, without a care in the world. There in solitude and silence he would be able to hear God's secret revelations" (no. 4).[8] After his conversion, we find Francis in the Carceri close to Assisi, in the Portiuncula and later on the mountaintop at La Verna. What drove him, though, was not fear of the world, but only the yearning for Christ, the thirst for God. This separation from the world had no negative character, but was simply a means of achieving a greater intimacy of communion with the Lord.

Distancing and divergence do not characterize merely the beginnings of Francis's spiritual journey. They are a feature that remained unaltered even when the young man from Umbria drew other companions to himself. They appeared to their contemporaries—as the *Legend of the Three Companions* puts it—as "wild men of the woods."[9] Their missionary endeavor at the center of society and of the church did not minimize their otherness.

Physical contact with those who are different is a constant challenge. The exponents of an alternative faith are disconcerting: they are uncomfortable to be with; they call into question our own way of being Christian; they even arouse ridicule and contempt. History records the reaction of those from whom Francis and his followers begged alms: "Sometimes they were pelted with mud; sometimes jesters put dice in their hands inviting them to play; others pulled at them from behind, dragging them along by their cowls. These and other similar pranks were played on them by people who considered them of no account and tormented them as they pleased."[10]

Just as in the exodus from society, so too after the return to it, the quest for communion with the Lord remained the one point of orientation for the life of the friars. The idea of apostolate and preaching was never decisive for the spiritual itinerary of St. Francis (no. 1066). Not even the foundation of an order was planned. Saint Francis wanted to be alone with the Lord: he wanted to have time for him, and to share all his struggles and joys with him. The conditions of life seemed to him of secondary importance; he did not concern himself with pastoral expedients. Still less did he develop any apostolic strategy, or devise forms of missionary activity or ways of protecting or propagating his ideas. He wanted only one thing: to share the life-style of Christ and live according to the will of God in uninterrupted dedication to him. Bonaventure reports that Francis himself was not sure about what specific form he should give to his commitment; this was why he constantly sought to shape and direct his community according to the will of God: "Eventually, they arrived at the valley of Spoleto, still full of these good dispositions, and there they fell to debating whether they should live among the people or seek refuge in solitude. Francis, who was a true servant of Christ, refused to trust his own opinion or the suggestions of his companions; instead, he sought to discover God's will by persevering prayer. Then, enlightened by a revelation from heaven, he realized that he was sent by God to win for Christ the souls which the devil was trying to snatch away. And so he chose to live for the benefit of his fellow men, rather than for himself alone, after the example of him who was so good as to die for all men."[11]

Although he did not retreat into a monastery or live in solitude, preferring instead to seek close contact with his fellow-men and their settlements, Francis conceived of the apostolate more as the radiance of a life wholly dedicated to God than as the assumption of an ecclesial service. To follow in the footsteps of Christ, who died for us all, seemed to him a proclamation of the gospel more powerful than any preaching ministry. For in total self-giving and in absolute obedience man becomes a wholly effective tool in the hands of God, who himself creates the salvation of mankind.

In so doing Francis raised an aspect of pastoral life that is of great importance, and one that is especially provocative for our time: the entering into the redemptive action of Christ through progressive assimilation to Christ by his imitation. In this way the apostle becomes capable of making Christ transpire in his life and the Redeemer present in his action. The necessary diversity or otherness of the witness, without which renewal cannot be achieved, is produced not by outward forms and conditions of life but by the apostle's greater closeness to Christ.

Francis lived this closeness to Christ in a community. The community was for him a kind of safe-conduct on the journey of faith. It is the school in which the faith is deepened. To be a part of it forms the basis and the guarantee for the strength and capacity to bear witness. In this bond with the community Francis reflected the medieval conception of man: man was essentially conceived not as an individual, but as a social being. It is always in the community, therefore, that the Christian lives his relationship with God. And it is in the community, in the local village as in communities large and small throughout the world, that the church has its undeniable value for the orientation of the faith. The biblical and patristic conception of the Body of Christ or of *"communio"*[12] is not difficult to convey, since it corresponds to the innate sense of life.

4. Seized by God

This understanding of man changed radically several centuries later. In the 15th and 16th centuries the individual's social bond was dissolved. He no longer understood himself on the basis of the community: on the contrary, the community had to give way to the expression of individuality. Henri de Lubac believed that this development has continued right down to our own day. It cannot—he argues—be reduced to a brief formula, nor can it be condemned categorically, still less circumscribed by precise chronological limits. The preeminence of the individual in faith and in theology, he declared, "evidently coincides with the disintegration of medieval Christendom."[13] This is not the place to describe the precise causes and wide-ranging effects of this process. It will suffice, for our purposes, to point out that the Reformation in the 16th century was not merely a reaction to ecclesiastical abuses. For in 1517 the church was in effect no more diseased than she had been one or two centuries earlier. Even before the Reformation she had had her great figures and impulses of reform, but hitherto the principle of community had never been touched, never been questioned. The individual's emancipation from it was the innovative feature that called into question the church herself. The German reformer Martin Luther not only abandoned himself to this new current of individualism but vigorously promoted and guided it.

The monk of Wittenberg was in turn driven by the fear of the wrath of God. Some Protestant theologians see in Luther's conviction that he was placed under the wrath of God the *Urerlebnis*, the primordial experience, of Lutherism. It is in this conviction of being the target of the Almighty Judge and Avenger, they argue, that Luther's key experience lies. He was tormented by the thought: Everything I find in myself, everything I do, is sin and is condemned by God. Even what appears to man noble and great does not stand up to God's scrutiny.

This conception Luther had developed with an unexampled gloom and detail in his exegesis of Psalm 90 (1534). He was convinced of his own depravity and could look forward to nothing but sudden death. Yet this prospect filled him with paralyzing terror. His only hope was that it might be possible for him just to survive. He sought words of faith that might show him personally the way to salvation. How could he escape the wrath of him who treads the winepress (Is. 63:3)? "How can I find a merciful God?"

The primordial Lutheran experience of sin, fear and divine wrath is one that the individual undergoes in his inner being. So preoccupied is he with this inner experience that his attention to the surrounding environment is diminished. He is oppressed by solitude. The Lutheran conception of the faith thus revealed, right from the beginning, a tendency toward religious subjectivism. This, in turn, accelerated the process of the isolation of the believer and the privatization of the faith. Luther wrote: "We are all sentenced to death, and no one will die for others, but each individual must be armed and equipped to combat with the devil and with death for himself. . . . Each individual must stand by himself in his place of battle and himself engage with his enemies, with the devil and with death, and alone conduct the struggle against them: I will then not be on your side, nor you on mine."[14] This expression of faith is all too revealing. The help that God gives through Jesus Christ and the communion with fellow Christians have been eliminated from the picture; fear of divine wrath obstructs a clearsighted view of the tenets of the faith as a whole.

Leading Protestant theologians wonder whether this key experience of solipsism and the solitude of the individual did not inevitably make Luther the destroyer of communion, and hence of the church herself; whether he did not inflict the death-blow on the church as a "supra-individual unity," even if he certainly had no deliberate intention of doing so.[15]

It is especially in mysticism that the church encounters the explosive force of theological individualism. For this spiritual current is, in the mystic experience, a way of legitimizing the disregarding of the communion of the church in the journey toward God. The individual person-to-person relationship with God appears as the Archimedean point of the life of faith, which cannot be called into question. The life of faith lived according to the principle of "God and the soul" is detached from the tradition, and can apparently dispense with the human mediation provided by the church's ministry. Interest in society and responsibility for it consequently wane. For he who is seized by God finds enough satisfaction in his experience of divine possession that he seeks no other.

The church, therefore, regards with great caution all those who relate to, or whose faith is impelled by, the private revelations of God. Only with great hesitation does she accept these phenomena.

Since the 13th century the current of mysticism throughout Europe underwent considerable growth: Clare of Assisi (d. 1253), Mechtild of Magdeburg (d. 1294), Gertrude of Helfta (d. 1302), Henry Susa (d. 1366), Catherine of Siena (d. 1380), Jan van Ruysbroeck (d. 1381), Gerard Groote (d. 1384), and the author of the first version of the *Imitation of Christ* were its best-known exponents. To be sure, the current of mysticism was nothing new; it could undoubtedly be traced in earlier periods. In principle, it would undoubtedly have been possible for the church to recognize the individual way of the practice of the faith, as exemplified by these mystics, and to make the so-called *devotio moderna* its own. Yet for a long time it was only the problematic aspect of all these seekers after God that was addressed—in other words, the threat they posed to the church as a community and the disinterest they showed in the church as an institution.

In Ignatius of Loyola God prepared a man whose mission it was to open up in the church an official way for the individual who wants to be conducted by God in person. The Spirit of God does not exclusively make use of the ecclesial community to make his will known; he may also enable his will to be grasped in the heart of the individual believer. The *Pilgrim's Story*, or *Autobiography* of Ignatius,[16] describes the renunciation and "expulsion" that he had to undergo. Only at the cost of suspicion and enmity could he open up to the church untapped sources for the deepening of the faith.

In 1526, at the age of 35, Ignatius came to Alcalà de Hernares, in the Diocese of Toledo, Spain, where he dedicated himself to teaching the catechism and, with the aid of his book of the *Spiritual Exercises,* to helping men to discover the presence of God in their lives. The encouraging response of Christians was quick in coming, so much so as to draw the attention of the ecclesiastical authorities.

In fact, it seems that strange things came to pass during these Ignatian meetings. The acts of the process of canonization report that, especially among the women taking part, there were those who reacted strangely to the preaching of Ignatius. "Very strange phenomena were produced in 10 or so of his female disciples, during the exercises (but also during the devotional meetings). They were covered by a perspiration of fear and lost consciousness or, losing control over their limbs, they fell to the ground, and, either wholly or partly unconscious, rolled about in spasms on the floor for an hour or so."[17]

It should be no cause for surprise, therefore, that the Spanish Inquisition should speedily have entered the fray. As an institution of the state church, it was their task to safeguard religious, and at the same time political, unity. The man with whom Ignatius had found accommodation informed against Ignatius and his companions, who were suspected and even threatened with torture. The inquisitors, however, strangely limited themselves to conducting investigations on the "greycoats," as they called the group around Ignatius, without interrogating them directly. The vicar general of Toledo, Figueroa, who then took charge of the matter, gave his opinion some time later that no error in the group's doctrine, and nothing wrong in their mode of life, had been discovered. They were consequently left in peace, and no measures taken against them, except for the issuing of instructions concerning their dress.

Yet four months later Figueroa himself reopened the investigation. During an audience three women were interrogated about the pastoral activity of Ignatius. Once again Ignatius escaped with no more than a fright.

In April, 1527, finally, Ignatius was detained and imprisoned. The prison regime to which he was subjected was a fairly lenient one, so that he was able to receive many visitors and even continue to exercise his spiritual mission as a pastor of souls. He remained there in detention, without being subjected to interrogation and without explicit charges being brought against him. It was only after 17 days had elapsed that the vicar general decided to conduct an interrogation. It ended with the decision to prolong the detention until June 1, when the saint was finally released. He was ordered to dress like the other students and not to speak on matters of faith for four years.

From Alcalá the silenced catechists moved to Salamanca, where, once again, they fell into the hands of the inexorable guardians of the faith. The Dominican fathers questioned Ignatius, who was accompanied by one of his followers, about the content of his Christian doctrine and tried to involve the two in theological discussions. Once bitten twice shy, Ignatius refused to give any information. The two interrogatees ended up in prison, where their legs were shackled together. The other companions were later taken into detention, too. Yet the interrogations failed to bring to light any theological errors. Three weeks later they were all released.

Similar experiences were suffered by the small band later in Paris (1535) and in Venice (1536), where the suspicion spread that Ignatius had earlier escaped the judgment of the ecclesiastical tribunal and subsequent handing-over to the secular arm of the law by flight. Not even in Rome, the goal of their pilgrimage, which was reached in November, 1537, were

Ignatius and his followers safe from enmity or suspicion. The Augustinian monk Agostino Mainardi, who had spread Lutheran ideas in his sermons in Rome, suspected Ignatius and his followers of heresy and, together with some Spaniards who had obtained influential positions in the Roman Curia, inflamed public opinion against them. It was only on November 18, 1538, that the tribunal of the Inquisition established the groundlessness of the charges leveled against them.

The same reaction described above to the attempt of Ignatius to renew the life of faith was to be repeated in response to his foundation of the Society of Jesus. "And they would not accept him" (Mk. 6:3). Ignatius was forced to leave, since what he stood for conflicted with current ecclesiastical practice.

Many other attempts at reform, other than those we have briefly mentioned, confirm this pattern of witness and opposition. Indeed, they almost turn the phenomenon into a rule. It is enough to cite St. Philip Neri and his Oratorians[18] or other founders of orders such as St. Alphonsus Maria de Liguori and St. John of the Cross.[19] Undoubtedly, opposition is aroused especially because the renewer is someone in whom God's witness always conflicts with people for whom the things of this world are important (Ph. 3:19), and thus challenges the earthly way of life of the church and her members.

For Ignatius the opposition was particularly intense, since the Reformation and its consequences had thrown the ecclesiastical authorities as a whole into a state of uncertainty; since concern for the preservation of the purity of the faith was clearly a pressing one; and since individualism as an intellectual current and the *devotio moderna* as a form of piety had seriously called into question the mediating role of the church.

The opposition to Ignatius cannot therefore be merely attributed to the short-sighted incomprehension or even the maliciousness of the church's leadership. Only those who lack a historical perspective will be quick to condemn them.

Historians have called the Jesuits "a kind of Catholic Salvation Army."[20] In effect the parallel between the foundation of a sect and the establishment of an order cannot be overlooked. When the Society of Jesus was formed around Ignatius on Montmartre in Paris on August 15, 1534, it might have appeared as a foreign body within the Catholic Church, but in the meantime the spiritual impulse of ecstasy and mysticism in Ignatius had been tamed to such a degree that it could be assimilated into the structures of the church. "The Ignatians of 1535 differed in kind from those of 1526, just as the Ignatius of Paris was not quite the same as the Inigo of Alcalà. Not quite the same and yet the same. . . . Eight or nine years are not a long time: Ignatius had cooled down, but he had not grown cold. There was still enough fire in him, when he reentered the public life of the church, to melt its frozen forms and rekindle its low-burning flame. The ever-repeated renewal of the church through its internal semi-sects, the orders, is made possible by the fact that the adjustment of the sectlike order to the low-temperature religiosity around it is only just beginning when they come out of isolation and go into action. This in turn is the happy consequence of the further fact, or rather antecedent fact, that the Catholic protest movements have always protested without becoming Protestants, that they have fruitfully bored from within, instead of fruitlessly attacking from without—and that they have been allowed to do so."[21]

NOTES

1. See for instance M.-J. Lagrange, *Das Evangelium von Jesus Christus*, Heidelberg 1949, who argues that Jesus' preaching activity outside Galilee essentially had the instruction of the disciples as its purpose, *ibid.*, 247 ff., 254 ff.

2. See H. Queffélec, *Saint Antoine du désert*, 2nd edn., Paris 1988, 131.

3. So one of the spiritual fathers of monasticism, John Cassian (d. 430), cited in G. Holzherr, *Die Benediktregel*, Zurich 1980, 51.

4. See K. Baus, "*Das Werden der Reichskirche im Rahmen des kaiserlichen Religionspolitik*," in: H. Jedin (ed.), *Handbuch der Kirchengeschichte*, vol. II, 1, 2nd edn., Freiburg 1979, here 17-30, 33-48.

5. See *inter alia* W. Dirks, *Die Antwort der Mönche*, 2nd edn., Frankfurt 1953.

6. Cited in: G. Holzherr, *op. cit.* (note 9), 268.

7. Letter to Eustochium, in: *Ausgewählte Schriften des heiligen Hieronymus*, tr. P. Leipelt, vol. I, Kempten 1872, 193-255, here no. 28. Cf. W. Stark, *op. cit.* (note 5), vol. III.

8. In: *Fonti Francescane*, Padua: Edizioni Messaggero, 3rd edn., 1982, no. 1044; Marion A. Habig (ed.), *St. Francis of Assisi: Writings and Early Biographies*, Chicago: Franciscan Herald Press, 4th rev. edn., 1983, 643.

9. Marion A. Habig (ed.), *op. cit.*, 926.

10. *Ibid.*, 928.

11. *Ibid.*, 654.

12. See P.J. Cordes, *"Communio* in the Church: Toward a Theocentric Understanding of Unity," in: *idem, In the Midst of Our World: Forces of Spiritual Renewal,* San Francisco: Ignatius Press, 1988, 153-183 (originally published in German as: *Mitten in unserer Welt,* Freiburg im Breisgau: Verlag Herder, 1987, 99-116).

13. H. de Lubac, *Katholizismus als Gemeinschaft,* Einsiedeln 1943, 274.

14. Martin Luther, *Opera Omnia,* Weimar Edition (WA), 10, III, 1 ff.

15. See W. Elert, *Morphologie des Luthertums,* vols. I-II (new impression), Munich 1952-1953, here vol. 1, 224-227.

16. On the following see the *Autobiography* of St. Ignatius, in: George E. Ganss, S.J. (ed.), *Ignatius of Loyola: The Spiritual Exercises and Selected Works* (The Classics of Western Spirituality), New York-Mahwah: Paulist Press, 1990, 68 ff. There is no universally recognized title for Ignatius's posthumously published account of his life. Ignatius himself dictated the work to his close follower Luis Gonçalves da Camara, but this narration was interrupted by Camara's departure for Portugal in October, 1555, and Ignatius himself never resumed what was to be his last work before his death in the following July. Camara left his manuscript without a title, and modern editors have invented a number of titles of their own, including *Pilgrim's Story* or *Pilgrim's Testament* and *Autobiography,* which, as G.E. Ganss points out, *op. cit.,* 58, "has by now in many languages come to serve as the most common title." It is the one used in the following. On the posthumous fate of the manuscript and early editions, cf. G.E. Ganss (ed.), *op. cit.,* 68.

17. Quoted in H. Boemer, *Ignatius van Loyola,* Leipzig 1914, 85 ff.

18. See J. Wach, *op. cit.* (note 5), 176.

19. See W. Stark, *op. cit.* (note 5), 306 ff.

20. H. Boemer, *op. cit.* (note 23), 57.

21. W. Stark, *op. cit.* (note 5), 387 ff.

II. "For building up the body of Christ"
Ephesians 4:12

Trust in God and the conscientious fulfillment of his will in the long run do not just move an individual alone: whoever gives himself to God with this purpose in mind always leads others to do likewise. He influences them, arouses them, carries them along with him. Seekers after God thus acquire companions. They form circles around themselves. They establish communities. They create a "movement" for others. The waves they generate are unsettling: they disconcert life in general; they awake it from dormancy and arouse it to action. The immediate environment is affected. Yet the sphere of influence thus created also extends beyond the local and historical context. Seekers after God are like earthquake epicenters, whose effects are detectable even over long distances.

This is why Therese of Lisieux has become the patron saint of missionaries: a girl who entered the cloister at the age of 16 and died at the age of 23, without having set eyes on, let alone worked in, even one mission station. For the church believes that the irradiations of the Spirit have, as it were, an underground force, and are capable of preparing the terrain for the seed of the word of God. She believes in the "deep mystery, and an inexhaustible subject of meditation, that the salvation of many depends on the prayers and voluntary penances which the members of the Mystical Body of Jesus Christ offer for this intention. . . ."[1]

The Christian who bears witness to the gospel can therefore be sure that his commitment and dedication will always bear fruit, even if not always tangible to himself: "spiritual energy" is never lost.

All too often, however, it can be shown that God has prepared the ground for salvation thanks to human collaboration. In outwardly tangible events God has shown himself to be powerful and to have intervened in history in a redeeming and renewing way. Here, too, therefore, the influence that reformers have had on the church needs to be addressed, even if only—for our purposes—in fragmentary form. It is once again history that will furnish our connecting thread.

1. The struggle against Arius

The father of monasticism found his biographer in Athanasius, patriarch of Alexandria. In this former Alexandrian deacon the first effect of St. Anthony, who, like Christ, was led by the Spirit into the wilderness, becomes tangible. For whoever took it upon himself in the ancient world to write the biography of another did not intend to erect a cultural monument to himself. A biography meant, rather, an act of homage to, and acceptance of, the personality described in it. A biographer wrote the story of the life of one man and brought it into the public domain in order—far more so than is the case nowadays—to inspire his readers spiritually, and to "transfer" to them the wisdom and values it exemplified. Athanasius thus conceived himself to be not just the biographer of Anthony, but his spiritual heir. He wanted to embrace the same ideals. He had chosen him for his model, and wanted to proffer him as a model to others. The fruit of the life and work of Anthony can thus be grasped in Athanasius.

In fact we find both men side by side in the most important conflict that the church had to face in the fourth century, indeed, one of the most significant ecclesial disputes that the church has had to endure in the whole course of her history.[2]

Already during the persecution by the Emperor Decius there was talk in Alexandria of the deacon Arius, who later became the parish priest of an important parish in the city. It was in Arius that the theology of an exegete, Lucian of Antioch, found its most successful propagandist. Lucian taught that, if the Evangelist John wrote "In the beginning was the Word," it must be inferred from this that there was a time when there had been no Word. Christ, therefore, was not infinite; the Son—Arius taught—had a beginning: "There was when he was not." This thesis speedily found numerous supporters. Many bishops, too, sided with Arius. The support he enjoyed was all the stronger since, to pagans and especially to Jews, the interpretation he proposed was easier to understand than that propounded by the church.

Such was the divisiveness of the dispute that Constantine feared for the unity of his empire. He therefore convened a council of the eastern and western churches, an "ecumenical general assembly of the church." It met at Nicaea in 325.

Arius, meanwhile, had not been standing idle. He had won over friends; he had developed his arguments. Yet he found a stubborn opponent in Athanasius, who had hitherto been a mere deacon and consequently without much standing. Still, the spirit of Anthony was alive in him and was communicated to the council fathers, who had confessed faith in Christ at the risk of their lives during the persecution. Solidarity thus arose between opposition to the demons and opposition to the Arian enemies of the divinity of Christ.

So Arius was defeated: only two of the 318 bishops at the council pronounced themselves against the *Symbolon* of Athanasius. Arius was excommunicated.

Yet he did not yield. He pursued his battle, even when Athanasius himself was elected patriarch of Alexandria in 326. He even succeeded in making the emperor change his mind. Athanasius then called Anthony to his aid. And so for the second time the desert Father left the wilderness to return to his native city. There—as his biographer Athanasius attests—he became a powerful and effective witness to the divine sonship of Jesus.

That the anti-Arian opposition of Athanasius was a matter of life or death for Christianity becomes immediately plain. Without his stalwart resistance, Jesus Christ would have been diminished into a mere earthly being. To be sure, he would still have been honored as a prophet, but one who would have spoken with his own voice and not with the voice of God. God himself would have been pushed back into the nebulous regions of the unknown, of the incommunicable—a God who had once created the world and had then retreated, without ever having shared a history with mankind. Undoubtedly, a God who loves the world, and gave his only-begotten Son for it, is offensive to rationalism; and Arius had the intellectuals of his time on his side. Yet truth transcends our petty calculations. It is not human, but divine. Athanasius of Alexandria preserved for us this certainty of God's abiding closeness to us and of his plans of salvation for us, which even the boldest human imagination cannot fathom.

Whence did Athanasius derive his strength? How did God

affirm and gain acceptance for the truth about his Son in the midst of the theological disputes and political intrigues of the fourth century? "What was decisive was the formation of a hard core of resistance, of a true center of renewal, and this we have to see in the ascetics behind and around Athanasius, in Anthony's men. They withdrew into the desert to steel themselves, but from there they released a spirit into the world which enabled the Church of the West to remain truly Catholic for more than a millennium to come."[3]

2. For the world but away from it

If we wish to discuss the role of monasteries or religious institutes in the West, we must sooner or later mention Benedict of Nursia.[4] He is in fact of unique importance for the historical development of Christianity in Europe. He has justly been called the "Father of the West," and Pope Paul VI entrusted Europe to his particular protection.[5]

Many will think in the first place of the great cultural contribution for which our continent of Europe is so massively indebted to St. Benedict. His monasteries truly became citadels in which the treasures of ancient culture were preserved. Without the care with which the monks safeguarded the writings and cultural values of antiquity, the greater part of this heritage would have been lost or dispersed. Yet, quite apart from this conservational role, the Benedictine monasteries became sanctuaries within whose walls enduring works of painting, poetry, music and theology were created. They survived as islands of civilization amid the barbarian flux of the Dark Ages.

The fruit that the exodus of St. Benedict brought to society and the church is thus incalculable. Books such as *The Name of the Rose* in many respects give only a very limited idea of this. The model of life together as Christians consecrated to God, as described in Benedict's *Rule*, has exerted an enduring influence on all religious communities ever since, and indeed continues in our own time to leave its indelible mark on the organization of secular institutes and lay associations.

When St. Anthony fled into the desert, he shaped monastic asceticism out of a combination of solitude, contempt for this world and prayer. The answer to the temptations of the devil consisted in a more determined solitude, a more implacable contempt for this world, and a more ardent pursuit of prayer. His spiritual ideal undoubtedly continues to retain its validity. Yet Anthony's spiritual strategy was later placed on a new foundation by an important element: experience teaches that the formation of communities can have a liberating influence. It was Pachomius (d. 346) in Egypt who was the first to proceed along this path.[6] Later, under Benedict, the living-together of monks in communities found a uniquely balanced form, which testified to great human and spiritual wisdom.

Yet, in the history of monasticism, the transition from absolute solitude to a half-eremitical or community life was frequently repeated. Benedict of Aniane in the ninth century, the Camaldolese in the 11th and Francis of Assisi in the 13th—all emerged from a period of solitude to return to human intercourse. Yet for all these men it was only by a great act of will that the abandonment of the undisturbed communion with God was achieved. Anthony did not hesitate to go to the aid of his native city Alexandria twice, but he did not remain there. Gregory the Great had difficulty in turning his back on his monastery, in order first to serve the papal throne and then to ascend it himself; and he has bequeathed us unforgettable words about his experience of intimacy with God in the secluded cell.

Yet the road back to society is important for enabling us to grasp the fruit borne by the renewers of the church. The continuation of a life lived in isolation would have made it most difficult for us to grasp that the exodus which took them away from society in the first place had borne a copious harvest. On the other hand, the reluctance to return shows that the monk is not a man in search of power. Authority is a burden to him, not a favor. In reality we encounter a paradox in the monk: "the paradox [of] a man who seeks to escape from the world, and yet is drawn back to influence, in a variety of ways, the world he sought to abandon."[7]

In 590 Gregory was elected pope. It was the will of the masses that made him assume his public responsibility. People held out the hope that he would use a broom to make a clean sweep of the church.

Immediately after the beginning of his pontificate, he replaced the controversial Arch-Deacon Laurentius by the honorable and highly esteemed Honoratus. He began his struggle against simony, the sale of ecclesiastical offices for money, a relatively difficult task, since the battle against the rich inevitably incurred the resistance of the powerful.

Yet Gregory did not fear to do battle. He tackled the problems of episcopal responsibility on a broad front. We may cite, first, his famous Lateran homily (*Sermo XVII*), in which, in his exegesis of the Lord's mission to the 72 disciples (Lk. 10:1-9), he lamented in no uncertain terms the propensity of the pastors of the church to succumb to the temptation of money. Second, there was his *Pastoral Rule*, whose aim was to serve as a mirror for the consciences of candidates for the episcopate. Third, there were his various appeals to patriarchs and metropolitans. Last, there were his innumerable ministerial decisions, aimed at holding back unsuitable aspirants to the hierarchy and at curbing various errors rife in the church. Step by step he tried to renew the church. When he died in 604, he left behind him a house in order. Gregory had renewed it—and the spirit of Gregory was the spirit of Benedict.

Of course, these impressive fruits could only ripen because Gregory had renounced the snares of this world and offered himself to the service of the church. He left the cloister, but the intimacy with God he had learned in it never deserted him. He continued to feel it so deeply that the yearning for the place in which he had experienced it remained with him like a constant source of pain. His service to the church, which forced him to remain in the world, thus retained the character of an exodus. His distance from the world accompanied him, though more as a nostalgic yearning than as an actual experience. To a deacon called Petrus he lamented the affliction and grief that oppressed him for having had to abandon his monastery.

"This daily sadness of mine, Peter, is always old and always new: old by its constant presence, new by its continual increase. With my unhappy soul languishing under a burden of distractions, I recall those earlier days in the monastery where all the fleeting things of time were in a world below me, and I could rise far above the vanities of life. Heavenly thoughts would fill my mind, and while still held within the body I passed beyond its narrow confines in contemplation. Even death, which nearly everyone regards as evil, I cherished as the entrance into life and the reward for labor. But now all the beauty of that spiritual repose is gone, and the contact with worldly men and their affairs, which is a necessary part of my duties as bishop, has left my soul defiled with earthly activities. I am so distracted with external occupations in my concern for the people that even when my spirit resumes its striving after the interior life it always does so with less vigor. . . . At times I find myself reflecting with even greater regret on the life that others lead who have totally abandoned the present world. Seeing the heights these men have reached only makes me realize the lowly state of my own soul. It was by spending their days in seclusion that most of them pleased their Creator. And to keep them from dulling their spiritual fervor with human activities, God chose to leave them free from worldly occupations."[8]

3. Signposts for the church

"Bernard loved the valleys, Benedict the mountains, Francis the towns," says a medieval song.[9] The verse pithily shows in what direction the first fruits of the Franciscan movement led. The "exodus" of Francis, like that of Anthony, brought dynamism and renewal to the church. In describing these fruits, it will be appropriate to begin with the improvement of pastoral care inaugurated by Francis.[10]

For a long period in the early medieval history of Europe, the towns and cities in effect coincided with the episcopal sees. Pastoral care was in the hands of the canons of the episcopal cathedral, to whom Yves of Chartres (d. 1116) had given a rule inspired by the spirit of Augustine. As is well known, Dominic served at first as a canon in the Spanish Diocese of Osma. Later, however, the town developed into an autonomous social structure: it expanded beyond its cradle and became removed—not always in a peaceful way—from its origins. At the same time the burning question was also posed as to the responsibility for pastoral care in the new centers of human life.

The tension between episcopal curia and city, founded in political dependency and the urge for freedom, was intensified in the economic field. To the inhabitants of the city, the church appeared as an adversary, not only because it presented itself in the trappings of feudalism, but also because it represented the money economy system that was being developed during this period. The cries of the poor were addressed against the lords who held the reins of political and economic power. For large numbers of city-dwellers these lords were in fact the local bishops.

Cities that were episcopal sees such as Louvain, Antwerp or Utrecht thus became hotbeds of anticlericalism. "The commune of Laon, which sacked its bishop's palace, dragged him out of an empty wine cask in which he had attempted to hide, and murdered him in the open street (1112), is by no means alone in its infamy."[11]

The response of St. Francis to such abuses was as simple as it was convincing: he renounced any political and economic superiority. He did so not, to be sure, for strategic pastoral reasons, but out of his boundless desire to follow Jesus and to live his gospel. His brothers wandered throughout the whole of Europe. They had no fixed residence, still less a fortified episcopal palace like the feudal bishop. In this way they could be close to the people, in the places where they lived. They shared their daily life and gave them an insight into their own lives. Their witness gained in strength, their word in conviction; for their way of life was itself a sermon without words. Their one true source of power was the word of God. They could exert no pressure, nor hold out the temptation of social advancement. They did not come on commission from the episcopal civic authorities. They humbled no one, but rather humbled themselves before everyone by begging. They were the envoys of a distant minister general, who was immediately subject to the pope. The gospel thus proved itself as liberation, and Jesus Christ was its sole source of wealth. The Franciscan friars enjoyed no benefices, no sinecures. Instead, they entrusted themselves to the providence of the Almighty for each new day.

Francis developed a new kind of pastoral ministry. In so doing, he, with his brothers, stood the economic and social order on its head. This inevitably challenged the reaction of those who had hitherto represented it.

In all this, Francis showed his church new possibilities. Moreover, by his own witness he opened up a way for many poverty-inspired movements of his time.

In discussing the political and economic conditions of the 13th century, we have already been able to glimpse the social tensions they gave rise to. The inhabitants of the cities emancipated themselves from their lords. But among themselves they were still split into an upper class and a lower class. Indeed, a kind of class war between the rich merchants and the propertyless common people raged within the city walls. "The new economic forms developed by the 12th century were producing confused masses with no accredited status at the base of the social order. These weaker folk were reinforced by an ecclesiastical proletariat; for clerical ranks, offering, as they did, convenient exemptions of sundry kinds, were badly overcrowded. So was generated what we should call today a class psychology. Among these people, disaffected, all but outlawed, arose various movements, proletarian in origin, inspired at once by independent scrutiny of religious values and by economic insecurity...."[12]

This scourge spread like wildfire throughout the whole of Europe and had as its consequence unimaginable devastation. Apocalyptic forebodings, engendered by social pessimism, intensified as a result. Peter de Bruys (d. 1126), Arnold of Brescia (d. 1155), Amanoy de Bène (d. 1205) and Peter Valdes (d. 1218) are just some of the men who reacted, each in his own way, to the century's upheavals. They founded sects, circulated heresies and fomented schisms, which sprang up everywhere like mushrooms in this fertile soil.

Who could succeed in bringing back at least some of them to the church? Christ, Lord of the Church, chose Francis of Assisi and Dominic as suitable tools, and Pope Innocent III as a wise pastor. In recognizing the community of the "wild men of the woods" led by Francis, this pope succeeded in ensuring that many of the religious movements of his time "worked in and for the church, so that they did not slide into heresy and become a dangerous threat to the church. Innocent III thus paved the way for Dominic and Francis: their papally recognized mendicant orders could become, in the framework and in the service of the church, the heirs and executors of the religious movement of the 12th century and deprive heresy of its sustenance."[13]

Yet it was not only for the church's pastoral ministry that the medieval mendicant movement proved decisive: it became a milestone for theology itself.[14] In the early Middle Ages monasticism was without any unified organization; the various religious houses each had their own form and organization, without any common or shared system of government. The individual communities practiced reciprocal communion through brotherhood and mutual exchanges. This situation was altered by the foundation of the Benedictine monastery of Cluny (910). Taking its cue from it, a recurrent structural model for monasticism was developed. From

Cluny it spread throughout Europe: from Burgos in Spain to Cologne on the Rhine, from the English Channel to central Italy.

Cluny had explicitly subjected itself to St. Peter. The pope's patronage at first offered protection against secular interference, but it speedily became a shield to limit the rights of the local church. Exempted monasteries arose, i.e., communities of monks for whom ultimate authority was vested not in the local bishop, but in the pope. Yet the Apostolic See had in no way founded these monasteries. They sprang up and attached themselves to it of their own accord, and provided it with a weapon in the conflict with the national and feudal particularism, by which the local churches and their episcopal pastors were held prisoners.

During the 12th century the heritage of Cluny lived on in the monastery of Citeaux, the motherhouse of St. Bernard of Clairvaux. From 1220 onward it enjoyed widespread diffusion throughout Europe and exerted a major influence on the conscience of the church. Not least, it contributed to the church a development which had influenced the experience and understanding of society since the turn of the 12th century: reciprocal contacts between people were increased and intensified. The crusades enabled many people to share the experience of a peripatetic life and acquire a knowledge of new countries. Lay people gained in social prestige both in society and the church. The hitherto pervasive feudal system lost power and ascendancy. Both urban and rural populations acquired new and greater freedoms. They banded themselves together in guilds and communes. A stronger sense of community, and a sense of belonging to an organically articulated structure, thus spread.

The new religious orders reflected the consciousness of the new society. They found an impetus in it for their own structure. They enjoyed a high reputation both among the people and in the seats of monarchical power. They spread rapidly, *pari passu* with the simultaneous social current of change, so that their special relationship with the pope also left its mark on public opinion in many parts of Europe.

Their leading theologians busied themselves in their writings with the bishop of Rome and his ministry.[15] Bonaventure (d. 1274), for instance, pointed out that the Apostolic See of the Church of Rome has received a threefold authority: first, it alone holds the fullness of all the authorities that Christ bequeathed to his church; it holds them not for the Church of

Rome, but for the church of the whole earth; all authority in the church stems from it and consists in sharing in its authority (*op. cit.*, 222). Albert the Great (d. 1280) argued, in turn, that the pope was given the fullness of power to safeguard unity and *"communio."* The keys to bind and dissolve are in the hands of the pope. Yet Albert does not see in the papacy a mere monarchy; rather, he sees the use of the keys in the hands of many: "To you as an individual I will give [the keys], which Peter [nonetheless] will not receive as an individual [but for a multitude]" (*op. cit.*, 231 ff.). Thomas Aquinas, lastly, maintains that it is not the power to ordain, but "the keys"—i.e., the power of the government and the knowledge (of the faith)—that was given by Peter to the Apostles and by the pope to the bishops. In the writings of St. Thomas Aquinas it would be difficult to find any conception of episcopal collegiality. He even goes so far as to affirm that it is up to the pope "to define what the faith says." In this assertion Aquinas based himself on the inerrancy of the church. The pope bore responsibility within it for decisive events and for the convocation of councils. The members of the church must therefore submit themselves to his directives (237 ff.).

The search for God and the obedience of Dominic and Francis thus constituted a powerful foundation for widespread renewal. The pastoral practice of the time received new and fruitful impulses from it. The medieval movement of poverty, which revealed a tendency toward sectarian segregation, found a way back to the church. Lastly, a new reflection on the papacy was shaped in the new monastic communities.

Its theological foundations were thus further safeguarded, and its importance for the church reinforced.

4. Recognizing God's will

In the case of Ignatius Loyola, too, it is not our purpose to present the fruits of "exodus" in any conclusive or comprehensive way. We will limit ourselves to a few brief points of more immediate relevance to our present argument.

We may begin with the response given by the Basque saint to the *devotio moderna*: the trait of Christian piety which had scarcely been felt until the 15th century, but which spread notably at the beginning of the following century under the impetus of the rise of individualism and of the Reformation.

This spiritual current did not remain unknown to Ignatius. Indeed, he was deeply influenced by it: the mental and spiritual make-up of his personality, and the circumstances of his life, formed, we might say, ideal presuppositions for the search for the movement of God in the depths of the human heart—as it had been experienced and taught by Meister Eckhart, Henry Susa and John Tauler, but also by the group of Dutchmen led by Ruysbroeck or the "circle of the Friends of God." The Augustinian monks, the religious order of Martin Luther, were also stimulated by this movement.

In the already mentioned *Pilgrim's Story*, or *Autobiography*, written down by Luis Gonçalvez da Camara, Ignatius described the conflict with the Inquisition which the pursuit of his piety involved him in. But the account also contains the key to the book of the *Spiritual Exercises*, in which he summed up the results of his personal struggle to achieve a lucid insight into the will of God in an account which could also be placed in the hands of others.

After the atrocious surgical operation he was obliged to undergo following the injury he received during the French siege of Pamplona (when a cannonball shattered the bone in one of his legs), while still confined to bed during his convalescence, Ignatius asked for something to read. Instead of the novels of chivalry he had requested—a mixture of sentimental heroic legends and piquant ambiguities—he was given Ludolph of Saxony's *Life of Our Lord Jesus Christ* and a collection of lives of the saints, the *Legenda Aurea* by the Dominican Jacopo da Voragine.[16] "As he read them over many times, he became rather fond of what he found written there. However, interrupting his reading, he sometimes stopped to think about the things he had read and at other times about the things of the world that he used to think of before" (*Autobiography*, no. 6).[17]

The solitary convalescent was evidently quite aware of his personal reaction to the reading of these books. For he notes: "When he was thinking of those things of the world, he took much delight in them, but afterward, when he was tired and put them aside, he found himself dry and dissatisfied. When he thought of going to Jerusalem barefoot, and of eating nothing but plain vegetables and of practicing all the other rigors that he saw in the saints, not only was he consoled when he had these thoughts, but even after putting them aside he remained satisfied and joyful" (*ibid.*, no. 8).[18]

Soon after having been wounded (in 1521) in the war between Spain and France, Ignatius already began to perceive an inner echo to his mental and spiritual preoccupation, and this echo increasingly captured his attention: he knew himself to be in the school of God. Gradually he was led to further insights, as, for example, at Manresa, where he happened "to see in broad daylight something in the air near him. It gave him great consolation because it was very beautiful." It had for him "the form of a serpent with many things that shone like eyes, though they were not." He felt a "great pleasure and consolation" in contemplating this thing, indeed, "The oftener he saw it, the more his consolation grew" (*ibid.*, no. 19).[19] Yet at the same time as this phenomenon manifested itself, the serenity he felt in himself disappeared. He was tormented by doubts as to whether he could persevere in such a life of prayer and self-renunciation. He lost his desire to take part in the Mass. This led him to conclude that the enchanted being he had contemplated could only have been an illusion sown by the devil himself (See *ibid.*, nos. 20 ff.).

It was through this meticulous self-observation, which he patiently pursued, continuously refined, and discussed with many "persons with experience in the spiritual life," that he was able to formulate a basic element of the *Exercises*, the "rules for the discernment of spirits."[20] These rules include perseverance and constancy for the time of desolation; the exposure of the machinations of the devil; the ambiguity of consolations; the importance of paying attention to the whole train of thoughts, and whether it tends to what is wholly good; the elucidation of the direction evil takes in the pursuit of its goals. In all this Ignatius had no doubts about whether consolation could be experienced. His point of departure is the assertion that it is God, and God alone, who arouses genuine consolations in the soul that has given itself to him (See the *Spiritual Exercises*, 330). It is thus God himself who gives signs of his presence and of his guidance in the soul of the man who has dedicated himself to him; he does so through courage, patience and joy on the one hand, and through affliction, sorrow and so-called aridity on the other. The appearance and disappearance of these moods are far more than a purely natural condition for the life of faith and the response of the soul to significant spiritual events: they testify in the soul itself to its relationship with God, and God seems to make use of them in the guidance he gives to man.

The spiritual significance of this observation and the pastoral value of the fruit of the Ignatian "exodus" are thus immeasurable. To be sure, Ignatius was in no way the progenitor of those who make a connection between divine revelation and human sensibility.[21] The letters of Paul are already characterized by this correlation (*op. cit.*, 216 ff.). And the Fathers of the church deduce from this interaction a variety of teachings about the experience of the faith (*ibid.*, 254-280). But it was Ignatius who was the first to describe in every detail what role the senses can play in the perception of God's will. It was Ignatius who first affirmed that man can let himself be guided by God with the help of the senses.

If, as Ignatius maintains, the motion of the soul of any ordinary Christian is not to be attributed to psychology alone, and the soul is open to the manifestations of God, it then follows that no separation can in principle be drawn between apparently insignificant states of mind and the depths of genuinely mystic experiences. A borderline must certainly be drawn between recognized mystics, who are qualified witnesses of God, and the rest of believers, but on the other hand the similarity between both modes of experience is undeniable. "The mystic experience is one that prolongs another experience: it does so by deepening and purifying, clarifying, transcending and culminating it. . . . Only if it can be shown that the mystic experience enlarges, if it does not initiate, the integral Christian experience, can it be proved that it constitutes no degenerate experience"(*op. cit.*, 288). It is thus not only the highly gifted and especially blessed who are able "*solus cum Deo solo*" to be profoundly touched by the truth of the revelation of Christ: each baptized Christian is invited as an individual to hear the call of Christ "in prayerful listening, in the actualization of the 'life of Christ' made tangible in the 'consolation' of the existential recognition of God's will."[22]

In his affirmation of the individual experience of God, Ignatius embraced the modern intellectual and spiritual current of individualism and the attempts to renew the faith deriving from the *devotio moderna*. It is not only those in religious orders or members of universities who can be led to spiritual perfection, by regularly devoting themselves to meditation and contemplation. Each individual stands in an immediate relation to God. Although Ignatius focused his attention on the individual, with a view to the deepening of the faith, and leaves the community of faith largely out of view, he does not abandon the individual totally to himself. In this regard we may point to the instruction that the giver of the *Spiritual Exercises* should not interfere in the dialogue between God and the soul; he should rather stand by "like the pointer of a scale in equilibrium, to allow the Creator to deal immediately with the creature and the creature with its Creator and Lord" (*Spiritual Exercises*, 15).[23] At the same time, though, the subjectivity of the individual must be accompanied by the objectivity of the ministerial church: the giver of the *Exercises* must verify, on the basis of the church's experience, the discernment of spirits which the exerciser has learned. In this way the verification of spirits is not exposed to the danger of becoming encapsulated or transfixed in the individual experience. It remains an experience in the context of the church, "an effort to develop something given, to discover something hidden, to grasp oneself in its mystery, in which the mystery of Christ, the Redeemer, is grasped through the church."[24]

The power of the intellectual and spiritual enterprise of Ignatius in the history of salvation is made abundantly clear by a comparison with the Augustinian monk Martin Luther. He, too, sought the path of individual piety. He, too, wanted to counter an exteriorized ecclesiastical practice by the deepening of the personal relationship with God. However, in so doing he dissociated himself from the existing community of faith, and ended up by absolutizing his personal decision: "To act against conscience is troublesome, pernicious, dangerous. So God help me, Amen." So reads the fundamental article he penned at Worms in 1521.

That the breach produced in the church by Luther was not inevitable is maintained by, among others, the Protestant church historian Adolf von Harnack. He judges the response of the Council of Trent to the Lutheran doctrine of justification in a wholly positive way, and traces it back *inter alia* to an influential "party in Catholicism" which could not "simply identify itself" with "the old nominalistic scholasticism"; rather, it "strongly emphasized" the "Augustinian mystic ideas—which acted as a counterpoise to the sacramental system—and . . . opposed Pelagianism and probabilism." Harnack goes on to develop interesting speculations on the historical course of events and deplores the delayed formulation of the decree on justification. He argued that an earlier and more intensive diffusion of "Augustinian mysticism" (and also, by implication, that of the Ignatian spiritual practice) could have prevented the church's schism. He writes: "Indeed, it may be doubted whether the Reformation would have developed if this decree had been issued at the Lateran Council at the beginning of the 16th century, and had really passed into the flesh and blood of the church."[25] Ignatius, therefore, gave the best answer to the problem that for Martin Luther ended in the church's schism.[26]

It is not only in terms of the individual relationship of man to God that Ignatius achieved a central insight into what it means to be a Christian. His commitment to the faith also led him to emphasize a truth of fundamental importance for the structure of the church—the papacy.

The *Autobiography* shows that he had consecrated himself to this institution very shortly after his conversion. From 1528 on, Ignatius was, with one or two interruptions, based in Paris. It was there, in 1533, that he began the study of theology. During these years his first companions united themselves with him: Peter Faber (Pierre Favre), Francis Xavier, Diego Laynez and others. This led to joint reflections and eventually, on August 15, 1534, on the hill of Montmartre, to the communal act by which the small group and its consecration to God were given concrete expression. During the celebration of Mass its members vowed to serve God in poverty, and to go to the Holy Land to dedicate themselves there to the care of souls. In case they did not receive an opportunity to make this journey within a year of their arrival in Venice, or in case they were not able to remain for any lengthy period in the Holy Land, they would place themselves at the disposal of the pope as the vicar of Christ, "so that he might use them wherever in his judgment more was to be achieved for the glory of God and the salvation of souls."[27]

This particular and explicit bond with the pope is unparalleled in the history of the attempts to reform the church. In the age of the Reformation it marked a conspicuous resolve. Its motivation and its meaning can be further elucidated in the light of ensuing events and of later reflections to be associated with this act of consecration.

In January, 1536, Ignatius went to Venice. His companions

joined him there at the beginning of the following year. They then learned that no ship was scheduled to depart for the Near East that year, due to the breaking of relations between the Venetians and the Turks. The small band interpreted this obstacle as a sign from God: just as God reveals his will in the reactions of the soul, so he enables believers to grasp his will through the events of history. Having waited in vain for a boat, the first Jesuits thus decided to direct their steps toward Rome (*Autobiography*, nos. 92-96).

In the summer of 1538—the deadline laid down on Montmartre had long passed—the 10 companions were finally all reunited again. In November of the same year they took the decisive step toward their subordination to the instructions of the pope. Shortly afterward, the tempting proposal of the emperor, that they should go as missionaries to the Spanish Indies, intervened, but the answer could only be no. It testifies to the paramount importance that the vow of obedience to the pope had for them. "All of us, who are bound together in this community, have placed ourselves in the hands of the pope, because he is the supreme head of the harvest of Christ. In making this offer of ourselves to him, we declared to him that we are ready for everything he should decide about us in Christ. . . . Why have we submitted ourselves to his judgment and his will by a pledge of this kind? Because we know that he knows better than anyone else the needs of Christianity as a whole." The companions thus remained at Rome, "because in Rome too the harvest is great."[28]

In his *Memoriale* of 1542, Blessed Peter Faber speaks yet again of this act, which is called one of "consecration." As always, it appears as an event of maximum importance for the Jesuit community: "It was also a particular grace, and one fundamental for our Society, that during this same year . . . we made the full offering of our lives to Pope Paul III. . . . Our Lord was pleased that the pope should gratefully accept us and be delighted with our plans." The author then continues in emotional terms to express gratitude to Jesus Christ for this vocation, and declares: "Through the voice of his vicar on earth (which means a quite evident vocation) he was pleased to strengthen us, so that our service may be pleasing to him and he may employ us in his service for ever" (*Memoriale*, no. 18).

What is striking about this is, above all, the fact that the community held itself to be totally in the hands of God. It is

God himself who leads their history. It was their one and only task to ascertain his will day by day, as he manifests it in their history. In this sense they live an all-embracing, all-pervasive faith in an exemplary way. This is how Ignatius, too, saw it in a letter dating to this period: "Since we have begun the work here, not once up till the present day have we had to miss the two or three sermons on feastdays and the two daily hours of instruction. Others are fully occupied with confessions and in giving exercises. . . . The hostility we experienced was very strong, but it would contradict the truth if we were to say that we have lacked work and that God our Lord has not helped us to a degree that far exceeds everything we could have achieved just with our own knowledge and will." In the post-script to the letter he once again requests larger forces for pastoral service: "May this enterprise be pleasing to God our Lord, for it is surely his affair. . . ."[29] Even in the excessive burden of work, Ignatius detects the ordering hand of God, and in the greatness of the task he sees the special benevolence of God, who gives them the chance to expend themselves in such arduous labors.

Yet all this was mediated by the person of the pope. The tone of Peter Faber's *Memoriale* is only comprehensible for those who hold the papal ministry in very high regard. Because of this high esteem it followed that the confirmation of their mission by the pope was equivalent to the certainty that God was with them and with their initiatives. Ravier rightly comments: the "surrendering of themselves to the pope is of the highest significance for the realization of their plans. It alone enables us to grasp that the Society of Jesus was born neither from a brilliant observation of reason, nor from the plan of a Catholic Reform. The decision of this hour rather follows the line of the events of the past and remains open to the events of the future."[30]

The submission to the pope as the vicar of Christ was aimed above all at enabling them to ascertain God's will, to carry out an effective apostolate and to achieve self-renunciation in the service of Jesus Christ.

The bond that Ignatius himself sought with the bishop of Rome will perhaps be a cause of special surprise to those who have some knowledge of the lives of the Renaissance popes. The church found herself in the midst of a society in turmoil, in the process of rapid change, and even its pastors were indelibly marked by this, in many respects, lamentable period. They were not only spiritual heads of Christendom, but equally concerned with the government of a worldly state, with the power struggle it involved, and even at times with preparations for war. Is it any cause for wonder that they were chosen by criteria that today would be thought scandalous?

What goes for the pope also holds true for the cardinals, since the pope himself came from their ranks. A historian of the period has written in this regard: "The Sacred College consisted of persons who were distinguished by their aristocratic lineage, by the favor they enjoyed at the courts of princes, by their ties of blood or other relationships with the reigning pope, by special abilities in the conduct of public affairs or even in warfare, and lastly by their humanistic culture and their taste for the fine arts. From Nicholas V to Paul III, the doctrine of the church, the theological sciences, and probity of life were not given the importance that is their due."[31]

What was a day in the life of such a man like? The same historian draws the following portrait of Cardinal Ippolito de Medici, a nephew of Pope Clement VII (d. 1534): "In the morning he buckled on his hunting dagger and spent the greater part of the day in fencing. He only wore his cardinal's robe when he was obliged to appear in consistory or in some public function. He was more often seen at the race track, at the hunt and in the theater than in his chancery or in church. At night he would stroll through the streets of Rome, accompanied by people infamous for their disorderly life and loose morals" (*op. cit.*, 10). A little farther on we read: "It was not thought scandalous that the pope should have illegitimate children, and that he should strive in all possible ways to promote them to wealth and honors. On the contrary, it was thought clever and astute that the popes should strive after temporal greatness" (*op. cit.*, 11).

These were the men to whom Ignatius totally submitted himself and his order! Clearly he cannot have done so by trusting to human greatness, still less personal sanctity. The Spirit of God must have revealed to him the supreme rank of the papal ministry. He believed in it. Otherwise the vow of obedience would have been deprived of all logic. The explicit subordination to the pope understandably had serious consequences when the first draft of the society's program (the *Formula*) was drawn up. It can be grasped in the first place by the fact that a recognition of the program by the pope was sought. The fledgling society therefore did not seek, in contrast to other orders or congregations, an initial approval merely by a local bishop. It followed that the destiny of the new order was dependent on the decision of a single person. Moreover, this peculiar characteristic of the society is also expounded in detail in the second chapter of the *Formula*. Each member of the society—and the order as a whole—was placed in a direct relationship with the pope. In this way a form of obedience was explicitly requested which transcended the measure of the due fulfillment of clerical obligations. The proposal of a special vow of obedience to the pope was precisely aimed at this "more," by virtue of which the members of the society were pledged "to put into action immediately, as far as it is our duty, everything that His Holiness should at any time dispose for the fostering of souls and the diffusion of the faith, without any equivocations or excuses of any kind." The authors of the document were very well aware of the particular burdens imposed by this obligation, which urged them to counsel prudence in admitting candidates to the society. Candidates would do well, it was urged, "before assuming this burden, to devote long and diligent reflection to whether their resources comprise a large enough spiritual capital to enable them to complete this tower (cf. Lk. 14:28), according to the counsel of the Lord."[32]

After a long period of waiting and the overcoming of obstacles, the *Formula* was approved in writing by Pope Paul III on September 27, 1540. The "fourth vow" contained in it can be understood as a spiritual guidance for the modern and postmodern age as a whole. The spiritual heads of the medieval mendicant orders had formulated the theological arguments for the primacy of the pope, but it was Ignatius who shifted the ground from dogma to spirituality. Inspired by its faith in the action of God in history, the nascent society applied the doctrine of the primacy of the teaching and jurisdiction of the vicar of Christ to all apostolic initiatives. Its sphere of application was thus extended. The will of God became tangible in the pastoral directives of the successor of Peter. An absolute personal subservience to him, and willingness to serve him, was thus his due. "For everyone ought to reflect that, in all spiritual matters, the more one divests oneself of self-love, self-will and self-interest, the more progress one will make."[33]

With this self-imposed pledge of obedience to the pope,

the Society of Jesus was able at the same time to recognize that, while the Reformation and its errors were undoubtedly to be confronted in the sphere of doctrine and the intellectual defense of the truth, that truth also has a need not just of correct theological formulation but also of apostolic proclamation. The doctrinal foundation of the truth is but a preliminary stage to its diffusion by credible witnesses.

NOTES

1. Pius XII, *Mystici Corporis* (June 29, 1943), no. 43.

2. See on the following K. Baus, *op. cit.* (chapter 1, note 10), 17-30.

3. W. Stark, *op. cit.* (chapter 1, note 5), 260-261.

4. The following is based on *ibidem*, 251-267.

5. See *Insegnamenti di Paolo VI*, vol. II, 606, of October 24, 1964.

6. See H. Queffélec, *op. cit.* (chapter 1, note 8), 193-202.

7. T.F. Lindsay, *Saint Benedict: His Life and Work*, London 1949, 187.

8. Gregory the Great, *Dialogues*, 1.1. For English translation, see: *Saint Gregory the Great. Dialogues*, tr. by Odo John Zimmerman, O.S.B., in: *The Fathers of the Church: A New Translation*, vol. 39, New York 1959, 3-5.

9. Cited by W. Stark, *op. cit.* (chapter 1, note 5), 28.

10. See *ibid.*, 280-285.

11. R. Bennett, *Early Dominicans*, Cambridge 1937, 4.

12. V.D. Scudder, *The Franciscan Adventure*, London 1931, 18-19.

13. H. Grundmann, *"Religiöse Bewegungen,"* in: *idem, Ausgewählte Aufsätze*, I, Stuttgart 1976, 50.

14. See on the following Y. Congar, *"Von der Gemeinschaft der Kirche zur Ekklesiologie der Weltkirche,"* in: *idem, Das Bischofsamt und die Weltkirche*, Stuttgart 1964, 245-282, here 259 ff.

15. See *ibid., L'Eglise de Saint Augustin à l'époque moderne*, Paris 1970, 215-241.

16. See George E. Ganss, S.J. (ed.), op. cit. (chapter 1, note 22), 19-26, 70 (*Autobiography*, 5).

17. *Ibid.*, 70 (*Autobiography*, 6).

18. *Ibid.*, 71 (*Autobiography*, 8).

19. *Ibid.*, 76 (*Autobiography*, 19).

20. Ignatius of Loyola, *The Spiritual Exercises*, nos. 313 ff. English translation in: G.E. Ganss, S.J. (ed.), *op. cit.* (chapter 1, note 22), 201 ff.

21. See H.U. von Balthasar, *Herrlichkeit*, I, Einsiedeln 1961, 123-412.

22. H. Rahner, article on "Ignatius of Loyola," in: *Lexikon für Theologie und Kirche*, V, 613-615.

23. Ignatius of Loyola, *The Spiritual Exercises*, no. 15; G.E. Ganss, S.J. (ed.), *op. cit.* (chapter 1, note 22, 125).

24. H.U. von Balthasar, *op. cit.* (note 21), 289.

25. *Lehhrbuch der Dogmengeschichte*, vol. 3: *Die Entstehung des kirchlichen Dogmas*, II, Freiburg 1897, 635.

26. See G. Chantraine, *"Ignatius von Loyola und die Reformation,"* in: *Internationale Katholische Zeitschrift*, 16 (1987), 506-512. The author refers to Rule 365 of *The Spiritual Exercises*. Here Ignatius subordinated the individual's freedom to the judgment of the church: "We believe that between Christ our Lord, the bridegroom, and the church, his spouse, there is the one same Spirit who governs and guides us for the salvation of our souls. For it is by the same Spirit and Lord of ours who gave the Ten Commandments that our holy mother church is guided and governed" (G.E. Ganss, op. cit., 213).

27. Ignatius of Loyola, *The Autobiography*, 85.

28. Cited in: A. Ravier, *Ignatius von Loyola gründet die Gesellschaft Jesu*, Würzburg 1982, 32 ff.

29. *Ibid.*, 34.

30. *Ibid.*, 33.

31. P. Tacchi-Venturi, *Storia della Compagnia di Gesù in Italia*, Rome 1950-1951, vol. 1, 1, 8.

32. Cited in J. Stierli, *Dokumente zur Gründung der Gesellschaft Jesu*, no. 8, issued on behalf of the Provincial Conference of Germany, Frankfurt/Main 1983, 25 ff.

33. Ignatius of Loyola, *The Spiritual Exercises*, no. 189; G.E. Ganss, S.J. (ed.), *op. cit.*, 166.

III. "A sign that will be contradicted"
Luke 2:34

That renewers of the church also pose a challenge can be grasped from the word "exodus" itself. It is undeniable that tensions arise when the Spirit of God provides the impetus for a radical faith, and Christians—often fumblingly—respond to it. Whoever loves tradition believes himself to be called into question by change. Whoever is impelled forward into new territory sees his efforts checked by corrective objections. Rivalries and partisanship are unavoidable.

It is only the word of God that gives reliable guidance on this point: "Why, then, do you judge your brother? Or you, why do you look down on your brother? For we shall all stand before the judgment seat of God" (Rm. 14:10). Scripture tells us that Christ is the Lord of us all. All the baptized live by virtue of him; they live and they die under his sovereignty. How then can someone condemn others because of their zeal as renewers, or because of their attempts to gain deeper roots in what has been handed down? Before the judgment seat of God everyone will have enough to do to answer for himself and to give an account of his own actions. Every judgment on others only distracts us from the more important duty of knowing and judging ourselves.

Unfortunately, the history of the church teaches us that Paul's admonition on this score has not infrequently been ignored as regards attempts at ecclesial renewal—also because the zealots of the faith have sometimes overshot the mark. Numerous obstacles have been posed if a group has sought to reincorporate itself into the ecclesial structure, in order to lead others to a greater commitment to God. A few examples will suffice to clarify this point.

1. Opposition in the local community

The experiences of the first Jesuits in Saragossa, and the conflict that arose there between the "reformed priests" and the secular and regular clergy, were diligently recorded by Pedro de Ribadeneira, who was one of the companions of Ignatius since 1540 and later his first biographer.[1]

Soon after receiving their earliest mission from the pope, the members of the Society of Jesus arrived in the capital of the kingdom of Aragon. There they founded a college and took up residence in various houses. Their apostolate reached many inhabitants of the city. The Augustinians were irritated by the fact that the followers of the new congregation were growing so fast in number. Among the pastoral clergy, too, envy was aroused. A member of the Cistercian Order, the nephew of the vicar general, lost little time in organizing opposition and soon won other religious to his side.

A pretext for intervening was sought and found. It offered itself when the reformers erected a chapel in the pastoral area to which the Augustinians laid claim. On the day of the chapel's opening they sent one of their members to the inaugural ceremony to put a stop to the planned celebration of Mass in the presence of the viceroy and many specially invited guests. But the reformed priests, and also the participants in the service, did not accept the protest. The dispute spread. The vicar general drew up an appeal to all the city's pastoral clergy. It was affixed to the doors of the chapel, and threatened with excommunication all those who celebrated the Eucharist or received any other sacrament within it. When this measure, too, failed to have any effect, the vicar general proceeded to excommunicate the members of the new order. As Ribadeneira reports, "they sang to them the psalm of malediction, they extinguished their candles, and fulminated against them all the forms of execration which are normally directed against the enemies of God and of the church." The reformer priests were thus considered by the people—Ribadeneira declares— "impious and damned." People avoided them in the streets. They did not greet them, and avoided all conversation with them. "They were forcibly expelled from the church by public abuse, because they had refused to obey the order of the vicar general" (*op. cit.*, 302).

The conflict became even further exacerbated. Saragossa was laid under an interdict, which would remain in force, it was threatened, so long as the members of the Society of Jesus remained in the city. The hatred of the population against them grew. To outlaw the members of the Society of Jesus even individually, unflattering portraits of "wanted poster" type were printed, containing the name of the person proscribed and embellished with devils and other grotesque details. They were posted in churches and distributed throughout the city.

Of course, many conscientious Christians in Saragossa did not approve of this persecution. Yet they, too, did not dare to contradict the authority of the archbishop or to fly in the face of the massed fury of the people. Things came to such a pass that, when a riotous mob mounted an assault on the Jesuit priests' houses with the aim of seizing their occupants, the latter were obliged to call a platoon of cavalrymen to their protection. Only in this way could a bloody conflict be avoided. Yet the intervention of the archbishop was still awaited in vain. The religious of the city were still not satisfied. Even the royal house sought no accommodation.

It was then that the members of the society remembered Gregory Nazianzen, who in the year 381 surrendered to his opponents, resigned as bishop of Constantinople and abandoned the city. They resolved to do likewise, and took steps to notify their decision to the Senate.

They used this communication and the surrender of the keys of their houses to present a detailed exposition of their objectives and the meaning and aims of their apostolate. They then gave the reasons for their departure. It was their mere presence that had led to blind opposition and hatred, but they did not want to be the cause of love being suppressed and of souls being ruined for whom Christ had died.

They then left the city.

In Saragossa itself, meanwhile, the rage against them died down, hostility evaporated, and, to their astonishment, some time later, they were recalled to the city. Evidently they had met the unjust opposition wisely and had shown how it could be tamed. What is striking in the whole episode is how they combined humility with self-respect.

2. Attacked by theologians

Groups of renewal in the church do not have to experience just the doltish aggression of incensed masses. Even in places where the forces of reason in the search for truth are highly esteemed, strong opposition may be aroused. This indeed is what the same order experienced at the University of Paris (Ribadeneira, *op. cit.*, 290-293).

Ever since its foundation, the Society of Jesus had left some of its members as students in this famous temple of learning. In 1554 they began to found establishments in other cities. The group of those studying in Paris had since grown to 12 persons. Yet they were still unprovided with a theological college of their own. Instead they lived as guests of Bishop Guillaume de Prat of Clermont, who owned houses in Paris and Billon and who had got to know the Society of Jesus during the Council of Trent.

Ignatius sent the Frenchman Pasqual Broet, together with a companion, to France to assume the direction of the order's two houses. At the same time the society sent an appeal to the king of France on behalf of its members. It requested that they, although foreigners, be enabled to enjoy in his country the prerogatives granted to its own citizens; in other words, a kind of French citizenship.

This plea was forwarded by Parliament to the theological faculty of the University of Paris. There the papal recognition of the order and the pope's letter were to be submitted to scrutiny, and a report made to the government. Antagonisms of a personal nature between one of the leading heads of the faculty and the Society of Jesus—Ribadeneira reports that the nephew of the professor in question had entered the order against his uncle's will—and other unfavorable circumstances concurred to spread unsavory rumors, to arouse prejudices and to lower the society in public esteem: "Our affairs did not stand high."

The result was that the faculty of the University of Paris issued a negative decree. Ribadeneira declared that its content "was so rigorous, severe and insulting that someone reading it and comparing it with the reality clearly recognized that it had been drawn up without knowledge of the truth and without understanding of the case."

The effects of the decree were not slow in coming. The members of the society were subjected to harassment, and a wave of persecution began against the Jesuit students at the university, and against the Jesuit priests in the pulpit. Protests against them were voiced by the people at meetings, by Parliament in its sessions and by the bishops in their dioceses.

When the founding fathers of the Society of Jesus in Rome

heard the news of this decree, they considered drafting a refutation. They began from the consideration that the condemnation of the society could only have happened because its authors had been the victims of errors and gross prejudices. It was also argued that a sober defense of the truth would not be displeasing even to the august scholars of the University of Paris, for had they not proceeded with the best intentions and with the ardent love for truth that distinguishes university professors above all others? Ignatius, however, disagreed. According to the testimony of Father Ribadeneira, he said in measured tones and with a serene expression: "I would like, my brothers, to remind you now of what the Lord said to his disciples during his farewell: Peace I leave with you, my peace I give to you. Nothing needs to be written now, nor is there any need to act, if vengeance or bitterness may result from it. Moreover, you should not be disconcerted by the authority of the theologians of Paris. I am convinced that it is considerable, but it cannot do harm to the truth. This truth can be avoided or combatted, but it cannot in the end be extinguished."

Ignatius, therefore, wrote to the colleges of all the society's provinces, urging them to request from the responsible secular and ecclesiastical authorities a public testimonial on the life, doctrine and practices of the Jesuits. The testimonials should then be sealed and sent with public authority to Rome. It was in this way that Ignatius, faced by the criticisms of leading theological authorities, submitted himself and his order to the judgment and protection of the Apostolic See. To anyone looking back at the pages of history, the conflict described above between the Jesuits and the professors of the University of Paris will appear a relatively harmless episode. Three centuries earlier, in fact, and once again in Paris, the forces of renewal and the university institution had already come into collision, and with such virulence and violence as to jeopardize the further pursuit of any teaching activity in the university. Father Ribadeneira makes no allusion to this circumstance in his biography, but it is surely beyond question that he cannot have forgotten the famous controversy about the mendicants.

In the years between the end of the 12th and beginning of the 13th century, universities in the modern sense did not yet exist. Education was pursued in the monasteries and in the cathedral schools. In Paris, however, a new form of higher education developed out of the cathedral school of Notre Dame.

Great teachers, such as Abelard, attracted young men from elsewhere. Some of them came from distant towns and regions. The Parisian school acquired an international character, and grew beyond the jurisdictional confines of the French sovereign.

At the same time, the need was posed to safeguard the physical well-being and civil protection of students. The civil and religious authorities, which at that time enjoyed supralocal influence and supralocal importance, thus came into play: "If the safety of scholars were to be safeguarded everywhere, if a universally recognized privilege to confer academic degrees, and, consequently, the universal recognition of these degrees and the rights they enjoyed were to be upheld, then the empire and, to an even greater degree in the light of the then existing relations of power, the papacy constituted the most suitable means by which such things could be obtained."[2]

Just like the members of the Society of Jesus, so the mendicant orders had found little sympathy during their great leap forward which led to their diffusion throughout Europe in the first half of the 13th century. The diocesan clergy mainly reacted to them in a mistrustful and hostile way; they feared for their vested interests. On the other hand, the day-to-day pastoral ministry they exercised in the parishes and dioceses was not exactly flourishing. At least, Pope Gregory IX in his bull *Nimis Iniqua* of August 21, 1231, expressed no favorable view on the pastors of his time: greed, envy and resentment predominated in many of them; the priestly duties were being seriously neglected. The priests exercising the ministry were clearly unequal to the new and critical situations of the period. Seppelt writes in this regard: if "the appearance of the sects" constitutes "a never deceptive seismograph of the church's situation, then that situation could hardly be called brilliant at that time, since innumerable complaints reverberate down the ages about the heretics and sectarians who seemed to fill the whole world and who had as their goal the subversion of the ecclesiastical order" (*op. cit.*, 215).

Apart from the general tension between the dynamic and forward-looking mendicants and the overtaxed secular clergy, it has to be said that the religious were better prepared for the meeting with science or with higher education in general. The secular clergy were signally ill-prepared for this task. They had been trained simply as country priests; at most they had attended a cathedral school. They were left to their own devices and more often than not given little help by their bishop. The religious, by contrast, came from the schools of their order. They attracted many youthful forces to their ranks. The provinces of the orders, which each had the right to send two candidates to the university, chose them from the best-qualified and bore their expenses.

The tensions thus fomented between mendicant friars and secular priests openly exploded at the University of Paris in 1252. The secular university professors felt themselves seriously threatened by the foundation of schools by the two mendicant orders, not least because they "had evidently subtracted from them a considerable proportion of their pupils."[3] The mendicants meanwhile had occupied four of the 12 chairs in the theological faculty. In a secret council the other professors, who came from the secular clergy, decided that henceforth each order could not occupy more than one chair. By this measure, which the college of professors (despite the fact that not it, but the chancellor, was responsible for faculty appointments) adopted behind the back of the religious, it was hoped to stop the advance of the new arrivals.

Notification of the decision was sent to Rome by the superiors of the religious orders. Pope Innocent IV then protested against the exclusion of members of orders from the teaching body, and annulled in advance any excommunication that would presumably be issued against any scholars who dared to frequent the schools of those prohibited from teaching.

The professors of theology from the ranks of the secular clergy realized from the pope's reaction that the sympathies of the Curia were clearly not on their side. They thus strove to exploit for their own purposes the aggression against the mendicant orders that had spread in many places. On February 4, 1254, they addressed a proclamation to all archbishops, bishops, abbots, general chapters and other ecclesiastical authorities, in which they attempted to justify the reasons for their actions against the intruders. It is manifest that in taking this step they had no scruples about defaming the religious or garbling the facts, for example, regarding the figures on the composition of the teaching body. Their spokesman, William of Saint-Amour, even went to Rome to plead the case of the professors belonging to the secular clergy. So successful were they in propagating their cause that they prevailed on the pope to abrogate his privileges to the mendicants and to reaffirm the restrictions imposed by the Fourth Lateran Council on religious, i.e., the authorization to hear confessions only with the consent of the competent ecclesiastical authorities; participation of the faithful in the liturgies of the parish church and the obligation to receive the sacraments there, etc. Nor was that all: on November 21, 1244, the bull *Etsi Animarum Affectantes Salutem* addressed a forceful reprimand to the mendicant orders. In it the pope listed the constant complaints made by the secular clergy against them: that they attracted parishioners into their churches; that they deliberately scheduled their liturgies to coincide with the times of the parish Mass, with the result that the parish priest remained almost alone in his church; that they heard confessions without proper authority to do so, and administered the Body of our Lord to those who had not been absolved; that they visited invalids with maximum zeal with the covert purpose of obtaining legacies from them for their order, and so on. For these reasons the pope once again enjoined the council's decisions (*op. cit.*, 99-101). The mendicant orders were dealt a serious blow, but not a lethal one. Innocent IV died a few days after the promulgation of the bull, on December 7, 1254, and his successor Alexander IV, a special friend of the mendicants, rescinded the decisions taken against them on the grounds that they were "too hasty."

The battle at the university entered a new phase when the professors of Paris not only attacked the position of the mendicant orders in the theological faculty, but also began to direct their accusations against the orders as such. The standard-bearer of the new assault was once again William of Saint-Amour. In 1255, with the support of the French bishops and some influential friends, he published a polemic under the title *Tractatus brevis de periculis novissimorum temporum ex scripturis sumptis*. "Couched in a vehement, passionately aroused tone, with a copious but tendentious use of the Bible, the book," writes Seppelt, "launched an attack against the preaching ministry practiced by the mendicants, against their practice of sacramental confession, against their propertylessness and mendicancy, against the neglect of manual work in the two orders, and against their scientific and intellectual pretensions" (*op. cit.*, 111). The difficult times heralded in the Second Letter to Timothy (3:1 ff.) had already, it was claimed, become a present reality with the mendicant orders. They were the pseudo-apostles and pseudo-prophets who—as Paul predicted—in the last days would insinuate themselves into people's houses; men who are self-centered and grasping, boastful, arrogant and disobedient. They were the proof that the Second Coming of Christ was nigh.

The attacks of the leading French theologian were all the more effective, since as corroboration of his warnings he could point to a text that compromised the mendicants. One of them, the Franciscan Gerardo of Borgo San Donnino, had written an extensive introduction to the *Evangelium Aeternum* of Joachim da Fiore (d. 1202), which contained numerous theological errors. This introduction was held up by William as exemplifying the theological conception of the mendicant orders as a whole. The professors of Paris backed him up by diffusing the *Introductorius* in excerpts, which distorted its meaning even further; this was at any rate the conclusion reached by a commission of cardinals set up by the pope.

However, the professors of the University of Paris were not satisfied with this partial victory. They continued their battle. They increasingly had recourse to dubious methods and polemical tactics that distorted or lied in the face of the truth. This is shown by a proclamation addressed to the pope on October 2, 1255. The pope, however, was not persuaded by their arguments. Indeed, he exerted his authority to protect the university chairs of the mendicants and the exercise of their activity at the University of Paris.

In an exhaustive study of this episode, Yves Congar has examined the theological positions of the chief actors.[4] They may be briefly touched on here. According to the interpretation of the masters of theology involved in this dispute, the biblical institution of the Twelve and the 72 disciples (Lk. 10:1 ff.) provides the justification for fixed competences in the care of souls and their assignment to determined persons. The priests appointed by the community exert pastoral authority over their flock. Any other minister is alien and foreign to the community. Not even special pastoral tasks admit exceptions to this rule. They are realizable precisely because God calls his ministers to them through the church, and so they are incorporated into the aforesaid God-given pastoral structure. Outside this structure there is no universal, permanent and unilateral mission. Anyone who, like the mendicant friars, arrogates to himself such a mission is in fact a false apostle, a "violator of the home," since he destroys the ecclesiastical order (*op. cit.*, 55 ff.).

This conception of the pastoral ministry in the church is essentially characterized by the territorial principle: a pastor of souls is competent for a particular area. Each community of faithful, each parish, has its *own* pastor. "The concept of *proprius sacerdos* plays an important role in the conflict over the services performed by religious after 1281" (*op. cit.*, 78). Evidently the professors of theology were incapable of conceiving of the church as a community of individual Christians. They were seen, instead, as an assemblage of concrete units of church members, which together formed a single structure from an amalgamation of local territorial components at the provincial or national level.

Against this static, immobile and definitively fixed picture of the church and of her pastoral ministry, the mendicants put into practice a supralocal, supraterritorial apostolate. In so doing, they formulated ideas of astonishing actuality in our own time. In their view, evangelization demanded auxiliary pastoral impulses, which needed to be harmonized with the old structures. Thus "the Church wishes to be missionary not only to those who are far away, to the pagans, in the way that the secular clergy conceive it, but to the Christian countries themselves, through a new and strengthened preaching activity, through the call to conversion, and through the celebration of the sacrament of penance. The mendicant friars were the men of a world in the process of change" (*op. cit.*, 146 ff.).

The opposition of the masters of theology in itself sufficed to realign the mendicants and reinforce their direct bond with the pope. An even more powerful impetus in this direction was given by their idea of an evangelizing mission that transcended the narrow territorial and local confines of the church. They thus found in the pope the ecclesial authority corresponding to, and connate with, the goals of their orders. In their world-view of the Catholic Church, they already professed in the 13th century the doctrine that would be defined at Vatican Council I, according to which the pope is invested with a universal, effective and immediate episcopal power. To be sure, Thomas Aquinas makes it clear that the title "universal bishop" does not mean that the pope is really and truly the bishop of all the episcopal sees in the world, since, if this were the case, he would eliminate the power of the other bishops. It means, rather, that the pope exerts a direct and comprehensive power in the church as a whole. "His jurisdiction thus directly involves all the faithful. They depend simultaneously and directly on the parish priest, the bishop and the pope" (*op. cit.*, 104).

By contrast, the professors of theology from the secular clergy had a minimalistic conception of the papal ministry. It is true that in William of Saint-Amour's *Collectiones* of 1266 the pope is denominated *tamquam generalis vicarius Jesu Christi, totius orbis rector et corrector* ("as it were vicar general of Jesus Christ, rector and 'corrector' of the whole world") and also *summus episcoporum et ordinarius singulorum* ("supreme among bishops and their canonical leader"). Nonetheless, William calls the other bishops the pope's "brothers and fellow bishops." It is not certain, therefore, whether he and his companions in the antimendicant dispute included the primacy of the pope in the dogmatic definition of the church. In their view, for instance, it was not an error of faith, but merely disobedience, to refuse submission to the pope (*op. cit.*, 70).

Yves Congar thus wonders whether it is not tantamount to extending to these men a terminology that does not belong to them to affirm that for them the church was above all a *communio* of particular (or local) churches (*op. cit.*, 78).

Church historians have lent support to the thesis that such an interpretation could have formed the roots of Gallicanism, i.e., the tendency toward a French national church independent of the pope. In some sense, this is clearly the case. For the university professors in question, authority in the church did not stem from its source in the pope. The Apostles, in their view, had received the same power as Peter, and in Peter himself it was the church that had received the promise of the fullness of priestly powers. The responsible canonical authority of the priesthood is thus vested not in the pope, but in the *ecclesia*. Within this church, bishops and pope perform a role of service. "*Vicarius Christi*" does not mean, therefore, that the pope is invested with the fullness of powers, or that he is entrusted with this by Christ. He was rather the head servant. "He has supreme power in the ordering of the executive (implementation), not in the ordering of the constitutive (institution)" (*op. cit.*, 148).

The mendicant orders, on the contrary, considered themselves missionaries of a diocese without borders. The pope had sent them everywhere to preach. Their mission was devoted to the one people of God, which embraces all the individual communities: parishes, dioceses, provinces. The pope had also given them the competent authority to perform it. Even if the keys were consigned to Peter for the church, and consequently belong to the church, the totality of authority still rests in the pope. He exerts direct canonical authority over every individual and over the faithful as a whole. He is head of the college of bishops, who have their authority *sub papa*, i.e., in subordination to the pope. In this interpretation, the theologians of the mendicant orders rested their case on Augustine, Jerome and Rabanus Maurus. In expounding it they held fast to the notion that the universal and supreme power of the pope was given to Peter by Christ. It was given neither by the church, nor was it given to the Apostles (*op. cit.*, 149 ff.).

No one following the current debate on the inherent rights of the local churches can ignore the importance or relevance of the theology of the mendicants for our own time as well.[5]

3. Examined by the bishops

There is no doubt that a community aimed at renewal in the church may experience the envy of others as a threat. Its vocation may also be damaged or impeded if it is opposed by theologians and condemned by authorities of the church's history and doctrine. Yet an even greater force of restraint is exerted by the reaction of the bishops. For the ordained leaders of the church are given the task of deciding whether the impulses by which a community was formed come from the Spirit of God; whether, in other words, a community has a right to exist in a diocese or not. Vatican Council II declared in this regard as follows: "Those who have charge over the Church should judge the genuineness and proper use of these gifts [i.e., those of the faithful], through their office not indeed to extinguish the Spirit, but to test all things and hold fast to what is good" (*Lumen Gentium*, 12).

Attempts at renewal in the church thus stand or fall on the judgment of the bishops. Their response to these new movements in the church thus calls for particular consideration. What position have bishops adopted with regard to the impulses of change?

Toledo

Let us begin with an episode described by Father Ribadeneira.[6] It has to do with the measures taken by the archbishop of Toledo against the members of the Society of Jesus. One of the most famous of the first Jesuits, Francesco di Borgia, former duke of Gandia, returned to Spain from Rome in 1551, and lived the life of a poor beggar. His preaching attracted well-known personalities and inspired them to enter the new order. New Jesuit houses were opened at Ognate, Burgos and Medina del Campo.

Archbishop Juan Martinez Siliceo of Toledo soon heard about the pastoral zeal and apostolic fruitfulness of the newly founded community. Since he was insufficiently informed about the legitimacy of its mission, he withdrew the right to hear confessions from all those priests in his diocese who had participated in the spiritual exercises devised by Ignatius. At the same time, he notified his flock from the pulpit that it was prohibited on pain of excommunication to go to confession or receive any other sacrament from these "reformed priests." Ribadeneira's account contains a comment on the founder's reaction to these measures: "When Ignatius heard of the opposition that so important a man of the church as the archbishop of Toledo mounted against the society, he turned to me with a serene and joyful expression, and said that he considered this persecution of the society to be an extraordinarily good piece of news; for it had arisen through no fault of the society. It was an infallible sign that God our Lord wanted emphatically to be served by the society at Toledo."

In the meantime the society, in its hour of need, had appealed to the royal court, which examined the documents of the order's foundation and the privileges it had received from the pope. It pronounced that the archbishop had acted against the pope's will and authority.

Pope Julius III in Rome had been informed of the dispute by Ignatius. The pope, in return, notified him "with apostolic rigor"—as Ribadeneira writes—how very astonished and sorry he was that the Society of Jesus, despite its approbation by the Apostolic See, should encounter such a rejection. In all parts of the world it had been eagerly accepted; only the archbishop of Toledo had opposed it and besmirched its good name.

On the grounds of this letter from the pope, and the royal

endorsement that reinforced it, the archbishop rescinded his provision.

Ribadeneira concludes: "I found that wherever our men were resisted with particular force, they were able to gather the most impressive harvest."

The intervention of the Apostolic See against the archbishop of Toledo's condemnation of the Jesuits demonstrates an important jurisdictional principle in the ordering of the Catholic Church. The bishop, indeed, exercises the ministry of unity; it is his obligation to foster and safeguard the unity of the faith (*Lumen Gentium*, 23). In the particular church that he represents he has ultimate responsibility for the doctrinal instruction and moral guidance of the faithful. Even so, he does not have it independently of the other pastors of the church. The local bishop thus remains bound to all the other bishops in the world. The local church lives by being referred to the universal church.

Looked at more closely, this truth means that "in the heart of each local church . . . the whole universal church is fundamentally present." Conversely, it also means that the local church is included in the universal church. "The universal church is thus not constituted as such by virtue of a federation, as if the individual churches could first establish themselves each on its own, and then later amalgamate themselves." The relation between the local church and the universal church is, rather, one of "correlation."[7] It follows that the ecclesiastical order is not simply to be equated with subordination to the local authority. Still less is the interdependence between the local and universal church to be conceived as a carte blanche for the overriding of the local authority.

This dual principle of ecclesiastical order ensures the church's pastoral ministry of concreteness at the local level, while at the same time safeguarding the local church from absolutist constraints. It is just this latter aspect that is clearly observable in the history of some renewal movements, for example, in the astonishing development that grew out of Benedictine spirituality—the Cluniac reform.

Cluny

During the Carolingian period, i.e., beginning in the eighth century, secular and ecclesiastical forms of government bore a very close resemblance to each other. Royal sovereigns were invested, like bishops, with priestly dignity and sacred authority. Secular power guaranteed not only civil but also ecclesiastical law. It defended the church, and acted as its champion. The power of the kings thus strengthened the authority of the bishops, who reciprocated by flanking the worldly rulers in an auxiliary role. Monastic communities and convents were not part of this structural organization; they were separate from it. They appeared as "islands of devotion and work,"[8] which strengthened the faith and promoted its social nature.

The aforementioned ecclesiastical form of government required princes of the church who were both devout and full of character: both spiritual leaders and worldly rulers. It was threatened by a weak or corrupt lord. This is why the crisis of the Carolingian Empire (mid-ninth century) also posed a threat to the stability of the church.

In Germany this danger was soon averted, but in France it grew ever more critical due to the powerlessness of the kings. The bishops, therefore, retreated from the court and began to usurp authority from the monasteries, which, to protect themselves from these depredations, sought the help of the Apostolic See.

The Benedictine Abbey of Cluny was founded by William the Pious, duke of Aquitaine, in 909. Ever since its foundation, it had sought protection from the pope, and expressly submitted itself to papal authority. It pledged itself to a new rigor in monastic life and to the reform of the church.

In a biography of one of its first great figures, Abbot Odo, we read that Adhegrinus, his close friend, had sought in vain throughout the whole of France for a monastery in which the Benedictine rule was conscientiously observed. He then decided to make a pilgrimage to Rome. Traveling through Burgundy on his way, he happened to come across an abbey in which the monastic life was lived in a convincing way. It was ruled by Abbot Berno (first abbot of Cluny). Adhegrinus lost no time in informing Odo of the fact, and the two abbots soon met (he eventually became Berno's successor as abbot of Cluny).[9]

The founding charters of Cluny leave no doubt that its establishment was dictated by a critical attitude to the church of its time. The abbey wanted to be, in St. Gregory the Great's sense, a "protest against the world." Cluny wanted freedom from the world, i.e., in the first place freedom from worldly power, but also freedom from worldly thinking. As the bearer of the spiritual heritage of Gregory the Great, Cluny represented right from the beginning an elective affinity between monasticism and papacy. This affinity already existed, therefore, before state-security relations and political calculation claimed it. Hallinger, an expert on the historical investigation of the reform of Cluny, writes: "The Roman trait is already to be found in the foundation charter of 910. This shows that even at the time of its foundation other ideal values and dispositions were already pushing in that direction. Odo and his hero Geraldus belong to the exponents of a devotional reform virtuously practiced *ab antiqua* in the Gallic area. Both made extensive pilgrimages to Rome, which, with particular reference to the cult of St. Peter, Odo wished to be understood as *pietas Christianae unitatis.*"[10]

It was for this reason that pilgrimages were made to Rome to visit, as Odo writes, the *coeli consules*, the "consuls of heaven." Here lay the spiritual foundation of the idea of reform, which was aimed in the first instance against the cohabitation of priests and the sale of spiritual offices for money (simony). At the same time, the "protest against the world" also repudiated any ecclesiastical and secular influence on the government of the abbey. Even the king was obliged occasionally to submit to rebukes and instructions from it (*op. cit.*).

The influence of Cluny continued to grow, so much so that the impulse it gave can rightly be called a "movement" in the history of the church. Many secular feudal lords opened the religious houses they had founded to the abbot of Cluny, and asked him to reform them. The abbot in turn received from the Apostolic See the permission to reform other monasteries and to readmit estranged monks to them. The charter in question issued by Pope John XI has come down to us.[11]

The tenacious determination to achieve reform and the abbey's growing influence did not procure only friends for Cluny; it also aroused hostility and opposition, such as that of Bishop Gauslenus of Mâcon.[12] At the French synod of Ansa (near Lyons) in 1025, he complained that Archbishop Burchard of Vienne had ordained monks from the Abbey of Cluny as priests without his permission, although Cluny was situated in territory under his jurisdiction. Archbishop Burchard replied that it had been Abbot Odilo who had invited him to the ordination in question. Being also present at the synod, Abbot Odilo then defended himself and referred in his justification to the liberties and privileges granted by the Apostolic See.

The local synod, however, did not accept this justification, and inflicted on the archbishop of Vienne the punishment of having to supply to Bishop Gauslenus a sufficient quantity of olive oil to serve as holy chrism during the lifetimes of them both.

After this sentence a direct appeal was made to Pope John XIX. He confirmed all the rights already granted to the Abbey of Cluny, in particular its exemption from the juridical competence of the local bishop, and the latter's prohibition to issue excommunications against Cluny. The same pope also addressed himself to King Robert of France, complaining that various French bishops had obtained their episcopates by simony. Not content with squandering their benefices in the pursuit of worldly pleasures, they had also plundered those monasteries which had been subjected by their founders to the direct authority of the Church of Rome. He, the pope, wanted to protect his monasteries, and Cluny above all, from the despotic acts of others. He granted to his beloved son Odilo and his followers the apostolic privilege, a copy of which he was enclosing with the present letter to the king, so that it might be read out in his presence and that of his dignitaries and endorsed by royal seal. Lastly, he threatened any bishop or prince who failed to recognize said privilege with spiritual punishments and with the loss of ecclesiastical benefices. Letters with a similar content were sent by the pope to Bishop Gauslenus of Mâcon and Archbishop Burchard of Vienne.

The papal reaction to the Synod of Ansa is only one example of the interest that the pope took in the movement of Cluny. Since the Apostolic See held its protective hand over Cluny and safeguarded it against any encroachments by the secularized local churches, the Cluniac reform could, by its example, help the resurgence of the spirit of the Gospel among bishops, priests, religious and lay people too. "The piety reawakened by [Cluny's] action and example, the concern for the salvation of souls, which the monks indefatigably urged, led many lay people to a purer and more penitent life and increased the veneration for the means of grace offered by the church. This explains why the dangers posed to the sacraments by simony and nicolaitism [transgression of celibacy] were so much inveighed against in these circles . . . and Peter Damian, one of the standard-bearers in this battle, knew very well that his adversaries were to be found not only in the ranks of the laity, but also among bishops and secular clergy."[13]

4. Cautious acceptance, especially by the popes

The short account given above of the Cluniac reform shows that the dual anchoring of ecclesial government—in the papacy and in the episcopate—has in the past had salutary effects both in the local and in the universal church. As far as Cluny was concerned, the forces of renewal could overcome local antagonisms thanks to the cooperation, not always free of tensions, between dioceses and Apostolic See. The principle of dual responsibility—local and universal—not only gave concrete expression to conflict, but emancipated it from the narrow constraints of local particularism. It could also prevent overly precipitate decisions which threatened to harm or impede the new reawakenings of the Spirit. At certain periods in the history of the church, at any rate, it permitted a "breathing space," a kind of moratorium, in which to purify the impulses of renewal and to scrutinize them in depth. Moreover, if the responsible ecclesiastical authorities allowed such a breathing space, this enabled them to lead back to the church even complex currents and movements. The medieval movement of poverty especially bears witness to this.

At the beginning of the second millennium, a situation of social and ecclesial instability pervaded the whole of Europe. Hotbeds of social and religious disorder flared up on all sides. The authorities could have reacted nervously and with the use of violence. Yet, surprisingly, calmness, flexibility and moderation prevailed.

Arno Borst, a noted expert on the development of the sect of the Cathars, cites the case of an Italian named Gandulf.[14] He set up as a lay preacher at Arras in France. He gathered around himself the largely uneducated common people and proclaimed to them there a Christianity of extreme otherworldliness: churches are heaps of stone; the ecclesiastical hierarchy with its church singing is useless; sacraments administered by unworthy priests offer no grace; nobody should marry, but all should free their flesh from concupiscence; the world and its snares should be shunned, and we should love our fellowmen.

How did the local bishop react? Gerard of Cambrai (d. 1048) sought out the community of Gandulf's proselytes, and pointed out their errors. He succeeded in convincing them. He thus won them back to the church.

Some 20 years later, between 1043 and 1048, a religious circle came to light at Chalons-sur-Saone. It met in secret and profoundly influenced the lives of its members. Their health had been totally sapped by prolonged fasting. Their liberty, too, had been severely curtailed by a series of theologically unsupportable ascetic prohibitions. They were prohibited from marrying, from killing animals, from eating meat. In a word, they appeared to be typical sectarians. What was the response of the church hierarchy? The competent bishop, Wazo of Louvain, eschewed recourse to the secular arm of the law. He preferred to attempt the recovery of these lost sheep and lead them back to the fold, through dialogue and his personal force of persuasion (*op. cit.*, 79).

The same pastoral patience is encountered in Pope Gregory VII (d. 1085), who was challenged by the sect of the Pataria (or Paterines) in Milan and Florence. This was a sect with a janus head: on the one hand it wanted to break the power of the feudal bishops and restore civil liberties to the cities. However, this liberation did not imply the abolition of all bonds; its aim was, rather, to remove from the church a burden which was foreign to her nature, and to confer greater force of penetration on her apostolate. Pope Gregory allied himself with those who urged a reduction of the earthly power of the church. In this way he prevented the Paterines from being pushed into heresy.

Pope Gregory VII provides a further example. In Cambrai a broad-based alliance of citizens and weavers forced the local bishop to grant civil liberties to the town. A priest by the name of Ramihrdus played a leading role in the disturbances. As a friend of the weavers, and a preacher of radical religious reformation, he refused henceforth to receive the Body of the Lord from an abbot or bishop tainted by greed. The local clergy, incensed, had the rabble-rouser sent to the stake. Pope Gregory VII, on the contrary, included him among the martyrs (*op. cit.*, 81 ff.).

It is on the pope's side, indeed, that indications of a more cautious, more forbearing, approach to those groups that pursued clearly ill-advised goals in their reforming zeal are recurrently revealed. This was shown, for instance, in 1162, when the archbishop of Rheims came across a group of Christians who were propagating undeniably Manichaean ideas and urging extreme forms of hostility to the world and the body on its members. The archbishop wanted to intervene, and together with the king of France appealed to the pope.

Yet the accused, too, sought to vindicate themselves and seek redress from the pope. Alexander III (d. 1181) tried at first to avoid a decision. He proposed providing the Flemish burghers with letters that would reinforce their position vis-à-vis the bishop, but they refused to accept this proposal. They insisted that their case should be decided in Rome and not in Rheims.

What happened thereafter is no longer historically ascertainable, but there is a revealing passage in the letter that Pope Alexander III sent to the archbishop of Rheims on this occasion. "The question whether the Flemish burghers are heretics or not he simply leaves undecided, nor does he give guidelines on how certainty can be achieved on the matter. He only warns in a general way against severe measures; for it would be a lesser evil to absolve the guilty than to condemn the innocent, and excessive indulgence is surely more suited to men of the church than excessive severity."[15]

Certainly, the exercise of patience and forbearance is becoming to an authority that sees itself challenged by innovators. Direct and patient examination of the question is a more appropriate response than the handing down of summary condemnations based on information obtained through hearsay, unless, that is, imminent civil unrest is threatened.

In principle, two groups of deviants are recognized in the sociology of religion: "Some sects have called for sterner and stricter principles of conduct; others have gone in the opposite direction and have experimented with far-reaching freedom, if not indeed with the abandonment of moral restraint."[16] Group formations of this latter kind can have subversive goals; they deliberately spread violence and destroy the civil order. In this case the church is clearly obliged to distance herself. She calls to her aid the forces of public order and speaks up for the cause of peaceful human coexistence.

Cathars

This at any rate is what happened in the case of the Cathars. In dealing with them, patience and benevolence would have been irresponsible. Their condemnation at the Third Lateran Council was not at all based on the sect's dogmatic errors. In directing sharp words against it, the council wanted to strike at this group because it had fomented rebellion and constituted a regular plague. It was necessary—even if need be with recourse to armed force—to reestablish peace and tranquillity in the land.

When the Emperor Frederick Barbarossa and Pope Lucius III met at Verona in 1184, and the pope obtained the intervention of the secular power in the struggle against the heretics, it was again not the theological but the social unrest caused by the Cathars that stood in the forefront of the church's request for assistance.[17]

Apart from the disturbers of the public peace, how has the church reacted to those currents which distinguish themselves exclusively by a rigorous proclamation of the gospel? How, in short, should the church treat radical but peaceful prophets?

Waldensians

In recalling the medieval merchant Peter Valdes, it should in the first place be borne in mind that the present-day Waldensians cannot be undifferentiatedly equated with the medieval group. The "poor man of Lyons" had no purpose of founding a new Christian community. His aim was that of leading his contemporaries to deepen their faith. He sought out fellow Christians with whom he could revive the mode of life and of the preaching of the gospel of the apostolic period, inspired by the ideal of evangelical poverty. "In simple woolen dress and without money, without care for the morrow, they made their way through the world, for they considered faith without good works to be dead. They formed no churches, but constituted only a band of itinerant preachers who shared the vows of Catholic monks" (*op. cit.,* 109 ff.).

The first Waldensians were therefore not the founders of some new sect, but agents of the reform promoted by Pope Gregory VII. The initiative of urging Christians to denounce simoniac clerics, and not to acquiesce in the lapses of the clergy from celibacy, had been his. In these "apostles" Pope Gregory's call for "a policy of moral pressure" against errant priests was given tangible expression. Something of this kind "by itself is not heretical and schismatical, or else we should have to call the greatest of hieratic popes a heretic and schismatic."[18]

In "exodus" and in the call for a normal way of life within the church, the hierarchy at that time thus saw absolutely no grounds for intervention. This is also shown, a little later, by the conduct of Innocent III (d. 1216).

He was faced with the unrest that the Waldensians had fomented in Metz in 1199. The local ecclesiastical authorities protested strongly and addressed an urgent appeal to the bishop of Rome, soliciting his intervention. The pope declined. In a letter to the local bishop, he expressed his opposition to drastic measures: "The church undoubtedly has the duty to catch the foxes that are destroying the vineyard of the Lord, i.e., to eliminate heretics. However, for the sake of this task she ought not to put true and unadorned piety at risk, or injure and confuse the religious sentiment of simple believers. What she must guard against is driving the religious naiveté of heresy into their arms."[19]

Humiliati

Even more evident is the "breathing space" allowed by the popes in the dispute with the lay poverty movement of the Humiliati.

They had spread in Lombardy in the second half of the 12th century. During the Third Lateran Council (1179) Pope Alexander III adopted an official stance toward them: while approving of their mode of life, he prohibited them from preaching on matters of faith. This decision was a bitter blow for the Humiliati. Had this been the final pronouncement of the church's hierarchy on the question, the innovators would in all probability have been expelled from the church. Yet the second successor to Alexander III reviewed the case. On June 7, 1201, he granted the Humiliati what they were striving for: they received permission to gather together on Sundays according to their wish; subject to the agreement of the local bishop, their members were allowed, during these meetings, to give addresses, which could treat of questions of the conduct of life, while avoiding those of theology.

This development is commented on by the Protestant

church historian Herbert Grundmann as follows. What had been prohibited to this group of renewal in 1179 was now permitted to it. The proviso that the licence to preach was subject to the bishop's approval de facto was hardly of any consequence. "For in the *propositum* regarding the Humiliati, the bishops were explicitly instructed not to refuse their assent. The holding of the assemblies was thus not dependent on the goodwill of the bishops; the arrangements with them concerned merely time and place." Even the exclusion of the right to preach on matters of faith was of no practical significance, since the Humiliati had hardly ever tried to obtain a licence to preach on such matters (*op. cit.*, 118).

From that moment on, the Roman Curia had few problems with the Humiliati, who in the meantime had spread in a remarkable way. According to the testimony of a contemporary, Jacob of Vitry (d. 1254), in the Diocese of Milan alone they had at their disposal some 150 community houses with an impressively large number of members. Thanks to the concessions made by the pope, it proved possible to reconduct into the bosom of the church the majority of those who had thrown in their lot with the Humiliati. Moreover, by this act, the church "demonstrated for the first time that she was ready to give up her negative attitude toward the [new] religious movements, and to accept the formation of religious associations of layfolk and even lay penitential preaching within the church" (*op. cit.*, 82).

Certainly, it cannot be forgotten that the popes lived in Rome. Geographical distance from the sources of unrest in itself may have fostered their greater leniency. It is clear, however, that this distance from the local situation also helped them not to be drawn into outward events, and to consider more attentively the elements of faith that lay behind them. The many ills that beset the church could not indeed be ignored.[20] It is precisely for this reason that the aforementioned popes did not seem to be mainly concerned with safeguarding the institutional order of the church at all costs. They recognized the justifications that lay behind the reform movements, and therefore accepted the transforming power of the innovators, so long as this was reconcilable with the truths of the faith.

God was already preparing the way for the man who would definitively lead a large part of this current of renewal back to the church—Francis of Assisi. "The truth is that the

Waldensians—and the Humiliati, and all the kindred groups, orthodox or otherwise—were overwhelmed by, and absorbed in, the great movement we connect with the Poor Man of Assisi."[21]

NOTES

1. Pedro de Ribadeneira, *Vita di San Ignazio di Loiola*, Rome 1863, 300-308. Pedro de Ribadeneira lived with Ignatius in Rome for the last 16 years of his life and, in close contact with the saint, gathered notes for the classic life of the founder which he later wrote and published in 1572.

2. F.X. Seppelt has described the conflict between the mendicant orders and the University of Paris in detail in: idem, *"Der Kampf der Bettelorden an der Universität Paris in der Mitte des 13. Jahrhunderts,"* in M. Soralek (ed.), *Kirchengeschichtliche Abhandlungen*, vol. III, Breslau 1905, 197-241; vol. V, Breslau 1907, 73-139, here 202.

3. A. Dempf, *Sacrum Imperium*, Darmstadt 1962, 336.

4. Y. Congar,*"Aspects ecclésiologiques de la querelle entre mendiants et séculéres dans la seconde moitié du XIIIe siècle et le début du XIVe,"* in *Archives d'Histoire doctrinale et littéraire du Moyen-Age*, 28 (1961), 35-151.

5. See P.J. Cordes, *"Die Synode über die Laien als Glaubensschule,"* in *Internationale Katholische Zeitschrift*, 17 (1988), 153-167, especially 164 ff.

6. See P. de Ribadeneira, *op. cit.* (chapter 3, note 1), 257-260.

7. H. de Lubac, *Quellen kirchlicher Einheir*, Einsiedeln 1974, here 43-54.

8. C. Violante, *"Das cluniazensische Mönchtum im 10. und 11. Jahrhundert,"* in: H. Richter (ed.), *Cluny: Beiträge zur Gestalt und Wirkung der cluniazensischen Reform*, Darmstadt 1975, 141-225, here 151.

9. Joannes, *Vita Odonis*, I, 22 (Migne, *Patrologia Latina*, 130, 3).

10. K. Hallinger, *"Zur geistigen Welt Klunys,"* in: H. Richter (ed.), *Cluny, op. cit.* (chapter 3, note 8), 91-124, here 123.

11. See G. Tellenbach, *"Reformmönchtum und Laien im 11. und 12. Jahrhundert," ibidem*, 371-400, here 379.

12. See L. Santifaller, in: *Römische Historische Mitteilungen*, Graz/ Köln 1958, 55-57.

13. G. Tellenbach, *op. cit.* (chapter 3, note 11), 395.

14. A. Borst, *Die Katharer*, in the series *Schriften der Monumenta Germaniae Historica*, vol. 12, Stuttgart 1953, 76 ff.

15. H. Grundmann, *Religiöse Bewegungen im Mittelalter*, Hildesheim 1961, 56.

16. W. Stark, *The Sociology of Religion*, vol. II, London and New York 1967, 184 ff.

17. A. Borst, *op. cit.* (chapter 3, note 14), 115 ff.

18. W. Stark, *op. cit.* (chapter 1, note 5), 333.

19. Cited by H. Grundmann, *op. cit.* (chapter 3, note 15), 100.

20. See also H. Wolter, *"Reform und Kampf gegen die Häresien,"* in: H. Jedin (ed.), *Handbuch der Kirchengeschichte,* vol. III, 2, Freiburg 1964, 197-205.

21. W. Stark, *op. cit.* (chapter 1, note 5), 334.

IV. "With the task of a new evangelization"

Pope John Paul II, July 6, 1986
Buccaramanga, Colombia

Christians believe that God has revealed himself, and continues to reveal himself, in history. They speak of God's acts of salvation through the centuries. They do so to exalt and praise his wonders at the dawn and in the early days of the faith, but also because past events continue to provide guidance for our own day. For their God is a God "not of the dead, but of the living" (Mk. 12:27): the same God who acted then still remains with them today.

Our brief review of the history of some renewal movements was not of exclusively historical or academic interest. The aim was not to display key exhibits from a museum of ideas, but to evoke the past because it has something of value to say for the present.

It should not indeed be overlooked that the fundamental ideas of these episodes of renewal were aimed at the apostolate, that their essential meaning was that of mission. The tree exists because of the fruit by which it is known. Yet this tree is of interest to us not just in its genesis, of which we have already spoken, but in itself. Mission depends on those who bear responsibility for it; it stands or falls by its nature and composition. The form of these movements will thus need to be tackled again, but this time with particular emphasis on what they hold in common. For renewal movements—beyond all the differences in the ways they were born and the ways they operate—all have a common source in the basic data in the Bible. They need to confront themselves with these data whenever their fruits are to be gauged. They are also exposed to the same dangers. Conversely, they may all take advantage of the same aids for the effectiveness of their action. The result is that interesting correspondences can be detected between their various forms. This does not mean, however, branding as unimportant or minimizing what is typical or idiosyncratic about each of them. It is presumed, indeed, that it is precisely in their common denominators that what is essential about them can be found: distinguishing features that clarify the forces of renewal and enable the movements themselves to confirm their action or prompt their self-examination.

1. The individual as addressee of the gospel

It is always the individual who stands at the threshold of any impetus of renewal or new beginning in the history of the church.

The Danish philosopher Søren Kierkegaard (d. 1855), with his unique lucidity and insight, raised our awareness of the dependence of truth on the individual. His writings date to the first half of the 19th century, but still remain of extreme relevance today. For Kierkegaard, the individual is the "decisive category in Christianity"; the individual, he declared, would "also become decisive for the future of Christianity." Kierkegaard's philosophical-theological reflection thus embraces and confirms the history of the attempts at renewal described above, though without making explicit reference to them.

In Kierkegaard's thought, the individual is opposed by "the masses," whom he evaluates in a decidedly pejorative way. While the masses appear to be decisive for temporal, worldly and earthly purposes, they are without significance for the ethical sphere, for truth. Kierkegaard indeed asserts: "The masses are untruth." He takes as proof of this the contempt for the individual shown by the person who aspires to place himself at their head. "Let him be accosted by just one person, a single man. What does he care about him? That is far too little for him, so he repulses him with disdain. There must be at least a hundred. If there are a thousand, he inclines to the masses, he bends down and makes a low bow. What an untruth!"

If the truth is to be decided by the vote of thousands in this way, then, says Kierkegaard, one should "express with the fear of God . . . that the masses as an authority, ethically and religiously, are untruth." Consequently, men must learn to become individuals again, in order to find access to Christianity. This is a noteworthy assertion especially in our own time, which suffers, as Philip Lersch says, from the "social overdetermination of the individual."

This high esteem for the individual receives a new motivation and a more marked emphasis in the perspective of the faith. That God is the foundation and guarantor of truth is, says Kierkegaard, more easily forgotten by the masses. "The fundamental confusion, which could be called the original sin of Christianity, is this: creeping from year to year, from decade to decade, from century to century—almost half not knowing what they wanted, and basically not knowing what they did— they have striven to deprive God of the right of ownership over Christianity and they have got it into their heads that they invented the race, the human race, even Christianity itself. . . ."

The philosopher compares this possession of Christian heritage by the masses with the circumstance that a piece of property without an inheritor passes, after a given lapse of time, into the hands of the state. In just the same way humankind had evidently concluded: "It's a long time since God, as master and Lord, has made himself heard, so that Christianity has become our property; and now we would like to disembarrass ourselves of it completely, or adjust it *ad libitum* as something that is more or less our property and our feeling."[1]

Kierkegaard could have known nothing of the dictatorship of the media and of statistics. This has made the masses even more "untrue." It has strengthened the obligation that Christianity feels is incumbent on it to reduce the gospel to what is humanly acceptable in it. Anyone who takes it literally is branded as a "fundamentalist" by the exponents of the masses.

Vocation

Yet, conversely, it is always individuals, not the masses, who have pointed in the other direction, that of God's truth and justice. This was true in the case of the Lord himself, and also in the case of those whom he individually called to his side during his earthly life. It may be that, even before this, it was also true of the followers of John the Baptist. In short, the call of Jesus was addressed separately to each individual.

When, soon after the beginning of his public ministry, Jesus gathered disciples around him, he was doing nothing unusual. Precedents and parallels for this can be found among the rabbis of his time—in other words, pupils (*talmidim*), who gathered together in the house of a rabbi and forged a close human relationship with him. They placed themselves at his disposal as servants; accompanied him on his journeys, following him at a respectful distance; and learnt in this way how to conduct themselves in obedience to the Torah. Above all, however, they listened eagerly to his words, posed him questions, and impressed on their minds, by dint of constant repetition, all they had heard from his lips. To be a member of such a rabbinical house meant being incorporated into a particular school, each with its own distinctive traditions and interpretations of the Torah.

The picture presented of Jesus in the Gospels bears a great resemblance to the practice of the rabbis. His teaching, too, like theirs, revolved around the exposition of the will of God. He discussed and expounded, like them, the meaning of Scripture and widespread doctrinal conceptions. He occasionally entered into a dispute over interpretation in the accepted rabbinical form. Indeed, he was addressed with the title of "rabbi."

Yet anyone who makes this comparison will soon discover significant differences. Jesus, unlike the rabbis, did not make use of a study house. Instead, he taught in the synagogues, in the open fields, in public meeting places, on the shores of lakes, and even during his wanderings. He appeals to doctrinal authorities or to traditional customs. His disciples, too, were never real interlocutors, or debating partners, who raised objections or expressed doubts about what he said.

The distinguishing feature of the teaching of Jesus consists, in the last analysis, not in the fact that he expounded the Torah, but that he preached with authority (Mt. 7:29). In other words, he claimed to express God's will independently of the Torah, and even dared to pronounce on whether God's will was really expressed in the traditional teachings.

Moreover, although the rabbis' pupils shared a kind of community of life with their master, it was considered from the outset as limited in time. One day it would finish, and the pupil would then become a rabbi in his own right. With Jesus, on the other hand, no end of the relationship between master and disciple is envisaged. He is and remains the master (Mt. 23:8), and the follower would also share in the fate of the master as disciple and servant (Mt. 10:24).

The contrast between the rabbis and Jesus is even more striking if the origin of the relationship between master and disciple is considered.

"Take a master to yourself, and you will raise yourself above doubt," advised Rabbi Gamaliel in the second century.[2] He wanted to say that anyone wishing to gain knowledge and understanding should choose a rabbi for himself. By contrast, a disciple of Jesus did not become so by his own initiative, by his own deliberate choice, but by the decision of Jesus. "It was not you who chose me, but I who chose you," says the Lord in John's Gospel (15:16). Others who wanted to join him were rejected (Mk. 5:18 ff.). They bear witness to the free gift of grace which distinguishes the call to enter the community.

Perhaps it is permissible to extend the vocation of the Twelve (Mk. 3:14) to all those whom Jesus welcomes into his community and who then become his witnesses. Cardinal Ratzinger describes this closeness between the Lord and his disciples as a life "based on this being-with-him," and declares that it is "in the being-with-him that the true place of existence is found." The mission to our fellow men has as its presupposition, he continues, the "practice in being-with-him, in existing close to him, in following behind him, in order to hear and see him, and be able to touch his way of being and thinking." This naturally ought not to lead those who are sent "to separate themselves, to exclude themselves from the ordinary day-by-day world." No club for the elite is to be founded; separation is merely a preparatory exercise for mission.[3]

Men and women set out individually in the imitation of Christ, which can only be accomplished by following in his footsteps. Christ was unprecedented and unique; he calls each individual in his respective historical moment. "Christ is among men the Individual, even the Solitary, *par excellence.* 'You belong to what is below, I belong to what is above. You belong to this world, but I do not belong to this world' (Jn. 8:23)."[4] The imitation of Christ can only be begun by individuals; it demands individuals. The individual encounter with the truth is irreplaceable: it entails the confrontation with one's own sins and the change of heart needed for one's own conversion. A sentimental blurring of our autonomy or its collectivist expropriation will not support us for long.

The eleven Apostles to whom the Lord entrusted his mission before ascending to his Father "were centrifugally dispersed" (*op. cit.,* 412). Persecution saw to it that bonds of attachment to the community did not impair their obedience to the missionary command to "Go into the whole world" (Mk.

16:15). Paul traversed practically the whole of the known world to share with it the cross and resurrection of Christ. From Asia he wanted to reach Spain, by way of Rome. On his travels, he continually established new communities, wherever he went, without attaching himself permanently to any of them. Before he was able to bring his plans to completion, he was deprived of his freedom and thrown into prison. He shared the fate of Christ: ". . . no one appeared on my behalf, but everyone deserted me" (2 Tm. 4:16). Individual commitment led to solitude. His blood had to be "poured out as a libation upon the sacrificial service of your faith"—the sacrificial service of his community (Ph. 2:17). The disciple of Christ thus came to share his fate.

Not only the apostle, but each Christian is irreplaceable before God, to whom "each of us shall give an account of himself" (Rm. 14:12). The community cannot substitute for him in doing so: "It is not through communion with the members of the church that the Christian enters into communion with Christ, but vice versa: it is in the individual's personal profession of faith and relationship to Christ that he enters into the communion of Christ's mystical body" (*op. cit.*, 414).

The recognition of these truths must be resolutely held onto, since it is precisely this "community" or "group" character of the renewal movements that is especially striking and is often emphasized. The considerable growth of these movements today is attributable in large part to man's growing need for community that is so widely experienced in our time. They are thus almost a necessary product of a particular spiritual outlook of many people.

This socio-psychological interpretation of spiritual movements may well describe something pertinent. Still, if absolutized, it succumbs to sociological shortsightedness. It dissolves the resolution and aspiration of the members of such movements, i.e., a force that is to be found in them precisely as individuals. These groups, despite their rapid growth, are in no way to be compared with an avalanche, which is released by a single individual, "snowballs" almost mechanically in size, and eventually becomes so huge and irresistible that it sweeps away everything it meets on its path. The community, on the other hand, lives by the commitment of the individual, in face-to-face contact. In this way it corresponds to the biblical model. Moreover, if renewal is spread by means of increased conver-

sion, then all the psychological and sociological aspects are rel-
ativized, and certain mechanistic forms of automatization are
eliminated.

Witness "in his Spirit"

The force of renewal grows from witness. In the first three
Gospels, we find indications of the fact that the profession of
faith in the Lord would inevitably entail giving witness to
judges and adversaries, in a situation of peril (Mk. 3:9-11).
Healings, too, were, in this sense, to be a form of witness and
arouse faith (Mk. 1:44).

For Paul, witness was bound up with the resurrection:
"And if Christ has not been raised, then empty [too] is our
preaching; empty, too, your faith" (1 Cor. 15:14). Yet the gospel
itself was also for him "God's testimony" (1 Cor. 2:1). The
apostle then becomes the agent of this "witness . . . to Christ"
(1 Cor. 1:6). In the original community of the church, the first
criterion of the apostle was that of being "with us a witness to
his resurrection" (Ac. 1:22).

It is this foundation of the service of proclaiming the gospel in witness that endows the Spirit with its capacity and
source. This was at work in Jesus (Mt. 8:4). It is the Spirit who
prompts the right words, the Spirit who speaks in the apostle
who bears witness (Mt. 10:20). The Spirit supports and sus-
tains the announcement of the mission of salvation: "We testify
to this. So too does the Holy Spirit, whom God has given to
those that obey him" (Ac. 5:32).

The theology of John sees the "faithful witness" (Rev. 1:5)
above all in Jesus himself. "He bears witness through his
whole life, for this is identical with his witness, that he is the
truth, the mouthpiece of the Father, and he can therefore say
with equal justice that, in speaking of himself, he is giving
sufficiently valid testimony (Jn. 8:14), because he knows
where he came from and where he is going, and because in
him two witnesses are speaking, the Father and himself (Jn.
5:13-14).[5]

Witness is always supported by the Spirit of God. In the
baptism of Jesus, it is the Spirit who testifies to him and reveals
him to John the Baptist as the chosen one of God. Therefore
Jesus, too, the one on whom the Spirit came down and rested,
would also baptize with the Holy Spirit (Jn. 1:32 ff.). In the

force of the Spirit himself the Baptist recognizes the Lord as the Lamb, and so also presages his end: "Witness through vicarious death with opening of the heart, which would be solemnly testified by the other John: 'This testimony has been given by an eyewitness, and his testimony is true' (19:35)" (*op. cit*, 377). Between the witness given by the Baptist to Jesus at the beginning of his public life and Christ's final laying down of his life as testified by the Evangelist, there is the self-witness of Jesus himself: Jesus who speaks God's own words and to whom God has given the Spirit without reserve (3:34). This enables him to testify to "what he has seen and heard" in the presence of God and hence *knows* (3:32 and 8:14). He is *the* witness of God (1 Jn. 5:9), who, in setting the seal on his witness through death by the water and blood of his heart, "handed over the spirit" (Jn. 19:30). The Spirit, water and blood are thus the common witness that spring from him and that bear testimony for him (1 Jn. 5:7 ff.).

In Jesus as faithful witness his followers have both a model and a companion on the way. They either fulfill the task of bearing witness "in his Spirit"—understood in the most comprehensive sense of the term—or they do not fulfill it. The work of Jesus is not dependent, of course, on the witness of his disciples. The Lord has no need for the witness of man. He has the Old Testament Scriptures that speak of him (Jn. 5:45 ff.); he has above all the witness of the Father (Jn. 5:36 ff.). Yet, in spite of this, he involves his followers. With his favorite Apostle, below the cross, he begins the service of witness of those who let themselves be taken into his service.

Imitation

Whoever is called in this way enters upon the imitation of Christ. It is this characteristic of imitation, in following in the footsteps of Christ, that distinguishes the relationship established with him, both in Jesus' own time and in all times.

The imitation of Christ may mean the relinquishing of our vocation or profession in this world: the first disciples abandoned their nets (Mk. 1:18), "they left their father Zebedee in the boat" (1:20) or the customs house (2:14) to follow Jesus. The bond with persons who have become dear to us is subordinated to communion with Jesus: father, mother, wife, children, brothers and sisters (Lk. 14:25 ff.) all come second to him. The imitation of Christ may also mean the renunciation of marriage (Mt. 19:11 ff.) and of all personal property (Mk. 10:21). The imitation of Christ determines, lastly, the renunciation of earthly power. It leads ultimately to the consequence that witness can only be accomplished in total donation, for the imitation of Christ visits the fate of the Master on his disciples.

"Foxes have dens and birds of the sky have nests, but the Son of Man has nowhere to rest his head" (Mt. 8:20). "It is enough for the disciple that he become like his teacher, for the slave that he become like his master. If they have called the master of the house Beelzebub, how much more those of his household!" (10:25). "But beware of people. . . . You will be hated by all because of my name, but whoever endures to the end will be saved" (10:17, 22). "You will even be handed over by parents, brothers, relatives, and friends, and they will put some of you to death" (Lk. 21:16).

In the last analysis, therefore, what Jesus requires of his disciples is nothing less than the readiness for martyrdom. He requires that the disciple should take up his cross (Mk. 8:34) and lose his life (Mk. 8:35); an unexampled demand that even the disciples themselves did not readily accept, responding to it by flight instead. Yet the infant church transmitted it in her Gospels, Christ's demands were not attenuated or watered down; on the contrary, they seem in the hands of the evangelists to be even more stringent and uncompromising.[6]

Not every Christian, of course, is invested with all these demands of the imitation of Christ in the course of his life. Even so, they are held up so that each Christian may imbue his life with their spirit. Anyone who exempts the Christian life in general from them, and restricts them to a narrow circle of ecclesiastical persons—as if the ethos of the disciples did not concern everyone—ignores what we have been taught by the history of how the Gospels came to be written, namely, that the gospels incorporate the wealth of tradition of the postpaschal Christian community. Even if not formally advanced, the demand for the imitation of Christ is intended as a provocation for the conduct of Christian life. It is a challenge to translate this imitation into a living reality experienced and embodied in particular situations; an impulse to an ever-growing self-offering. This is possible because every form of the imitation of Christ never springs from the disciple's self-willed decision, but has its source and foundation in God's call. Nor should we seek to dissuade or deprecate the radical nature of the imitation of Christ practiced by those who seek communion with the Lord in the renewal movements. Renewal cannot be achieved with faint hearts, for it is already sufficiently threatened by all the attempts to level down, or disarm, the provocateur and make him conform.

The word of Jesus and the example of the disciples unequivocally teach that evangelism is accomplished by the force of imitation. It is the persuasiveness of the apostle's life that wins people over to the gospel of redemption. Theological knowledge and pastoral expertise take second place.

This affirmation can diminish the importance neither of the ecclesiastical institutions nor of knowledge of the faith. About the meaning of institutions we have been taught much by the sociology of knowledge and of organization. According to its findings, man needs institutions for his own relief. They free the individual from the burden of having constantly to take a decision at every step—for instance, in the world of law, of health or of politics. Judges, doctors and ministers give us relative security as regard the fields of life they represent. Institutions, therefore, continue to operate in society because they are recognized as a "'permanent' solution to a 'permanent' problem.'"[7] Nor can the need for knowledge of the faith be denied. Theologians rightly assure us that God's revelation has transmitted a given content to us, and that this content needs to be accepted and penetrated by the vigilant exercise of the intellect. The person who really loves also wants to understand and will never cease to pose questions.

Nonetheless, it has to be recognized that the proclamation of the gospel runs into a limitation as soon as institutional and professional forces, i.e., mere expertise, gain the upper hand. Professionalism develops a technique which provides a convenient shield against the person's animating impulses. Careerism, both in thought and action, takes the place of more authentic motivations. The capacity to bear witness is stunted.

It is certainly not by chance that the development of the ordained ministry in the early church was only accomplished very slowly, and that its New Testament traces were only discovered with a great deal of effort. The importance of the sacrament of Holy Orders, ever more clearly apparent under the breath of the Spirit, undoubtedly led also to the risk of the members of the church being unjustifiably and detrimentally exonerated from their responsibility for the church's mission, a fact that in no way diminishes the ministry's biblical and dogmatic legitimacy.[8]

In saying this, it is not part of my present purpose to tackle the question—so frequently raised today—of the participation of the members of the church. If the church is understood as *communio*, no debate on power sharing exists in it; for "There is no limit to love's forbearance" (1 Cor. 13:7). What is at issue, rather, is the danger that the members of the church should believe themselves to be exonerated from their obligation to bear witness to the gospel; that they should persuade themselves that the Pauline admonition, "Woe to me if I do not preach [the gospel]!" (1 Cor. 9:16), is addressed only to the ordained.

The proclamation of the gospel through the imitation of Christ makes it absurd to rely exclusively on the formulation of programs and concepts, the establishment of institutes and the drawing up of curricula in the pursuit of evangelization. Anyone who limits himself just to these methods acts in a doubly shortsighted way. Evangelism is not a social process, to be prepared and implemented according to bureaucratic models; it must spring from people's hearts. What is decisive for it is not a knowledge of the subject, but a readiness for the unconditional imitation of Christ. This is a principle confirmed by the stronger propagation of the faith achieved by the renewal movements.

For those who are willing to listen to it, the call of Jesus means, therefore, total commitment. The imitation of Christ cannot be replaced by some organizational surrogate or delegated to some collective structure. It always demands the disciple in person. The obligation to bear personal witness culminates in the total donation of existence. It is death that ultimately makes the witness credible (Mt. 10:37-39). "No distinction should therefore be drawn between the total commitment of life and the witness of blood; evaluated from the viewpoint of the gospel, he who would later come to be called martyr is no more important than he whose whole existence means 'being slain all the day long' (Rm. 8:36; 2 Cor. 4: 10–11)."[9]

The saints have pursued this path of solitary witness—as individuals. Thanks to their obedience to the Spirit, the church acquired new strength. Teresa of Avila (d. 1583) reformed the Carmel and gathered new and resurgent forces in the church to counter the Protestant exodus. Bartolome de Las Casas (d. 1566) combatted the Emperor Charles V to ensure a more humane and just treatment of the South American Indians, and to impel the Christian emperor's recognition that love for our fellow men, and not military conquest, is the proper means of evangelism. Peter Claver (d. 1654) chose to become a "slave of slaves" in Cartagena to alleviate their inhuman lot and enable them to share the consolation of the suffering Lord. In our own time, Maximilian Kolbe, Dietrich Bonhoeffer and Alfred Delp have all, by word and deed, made God's love for man tangible in the most appalling conditions of prisons and concentration camps full of human evil.

In his account of the imitation of Christ and what it means, Hans Urs von Balthasar adds something on the goal it should serve: Jesus is the revelation of the paternal and trinitarian love. "Obediently, accepting even death" (Ph. 2:8), he willed that the love of the Father be made manifest in the world and for the world. The prophecy of the cross was fulfilled in the life and death of the first follower of Jesus, after his renunciation of self-love and banishing of fear had raised him to the recognition of God's great love. "The individual's personal witness of life is therefore, by Christ's express will, first and foremost the realization of brotherly love within the church, by which the church as a whole bears witness before the world and on behalf of the world to the love of God in Christ" (*op cit.*, 379).

2. Faith in community

The salvific action of God in Jesus Christ holds good for everyone. Its appeal to the acceptance of the gospel—in contrast to a long-distance call—cannot be "switched"; each must answer for himself. Yet in doing so the individual is not of course isolated, nor abandoned to himself. In all his capabilities, in all his needs, he depends on the gifts of others.

Indeed he depends on them even more so by virtue of being a believer. A telling affirmation of this can be found in the conclusion Dietrich Bonhoeffer drew from his experiences in the seminary of Finkenwalde and described in his *Common Life*: "The Christian therefore needs the fellow Christian who tells him the word of God. He needs him whenever he is uncertain and discouraged; for he cannot help himself alone without betraying himself over the truth. He needs his brother as the bearer and proclaimer of God's message of salvation. He needs his brother just for Jesus' sake. The Christ in his own heart is weaker than the Christ in the word of his brother; the one is uncertain, the other certain. This explains at the same time the aim of every Christian community: Christians meet one another as bringers of the message of salvation."[10]

In tackling the question of the apostolate, therefore, our attention must necessarily be addressed to the community.

Common priesthood

The church is more than the sum of individual believers. It is in the network of her relationships that the Christian experiences his bond with God. Moreover, the church is the historical presupposition and present-day foundation of the bond that unites the believer to the Lord. This is illustrated, for instance, by the famous passage declaring the community of believers to be "chosen and precious" and a "holy priesthood" (1 Pt. 2:5-9).

In this passage it has been pointed out by the exegetes[11] that the word "priesthood" deserves particular attention, since it is pregnant with great theological significance. The author of the First Letter of Peter, in enunciating this concept, refers back to the "eagle saying" in the book of Exodus (Ex. 19:4 ff.), which he consulted in the Greek translation of the Septuagint. He thus adopts the otherwise unusual Greek term *"hierateuma,"* (which was specially invented in Alexandria in the preparation of the Greek version of the Old Testament), in order to underline the community aspect of the group of persons described. The corporate character of the people of God was thus highlighted, though the individual's importance as member and coparticipant of the community mission remained intact.

By coining this expression in the pagan diaspora of the third century B.C., the translators of the Septuagint evidently wished to reawaken the missionary forces of Israel. The aim of the First Letter of Peter is identical. The line of demarcation is clearly placed between those who show "obedience to the truth" (1:22) and those who still remain outsiders. It fences off from this world the visitors and pilgrims (2:11) as the people who belong to God. This people is distinguished above all by a special kind of reciprocal relationship and by a different ethos. It thus remains "in concrete opposition to the world"

(Kasemann) and is not dissolved in the community structure from which the state, the *polis*, is formed.

The people of God, however, does not entrench itself behind a protective rampart, in order to defend itself from the rest of the community. The ties of faith that link it with its brothers and sisters within the people of God itself do not preclude an opening to the world. On the contrary, the acceptance of the call necessarily leads the follower of Christ to devotion to all his fellow men. The chosen have the duty to testify in their own lives to the holy One "who called you" (1:15). Previously they had been imprisoned by "futile conduct, handed on by your ancestors" (1:18); then they were called "from darkness into his wonderful light" (2:9). Although God is absolute holiness, he did not turn away from sinning men, but called them, though they were sinners. Now the act of the saint permits and determines the act of those God called. It is their task, like his, to lead the separated back to the fold by their own holiness.

The corporate character of this priesthood thus consists in a community that is closed in rank around Christ at its center and yet remains open to the world. The consequence of this is manifest: it is from the "living and abiding word of God" that Christians have been "born anew" (1:23), by which they are enabled to love like brothers, in sincerity (1:22). If they never cease to "love one another intensely from a [pure] heart" (*ibid.*), then their witness and proclamation of the gospel will also be credible. For it is the witness that flows from the individual's word and deed that is indispensable for the transmission of this word to others. The conjunction of blameless conduct among pagans and "good works" (2:12) transcends, in its effect, the confines of the community of believers. Corporate witness by the holy people of God leads outsiders toward it. The community that is formed around the Lord thus holds up a mirror to its benevolence and goodness, which also wins pagans to it.

A similar biblical methodology for evangelism is frequently attested today in the spiritual movements, and repudiates all those who hope they can achieve a growth in ecclesial credibility by their wounding attacks on fellow Christians. The Bible is unfamiliar with self-publicizing mud-slinging between Christians; at the most it testifies to opposing adversaries to their face (e.g., Paul to Cephas in Galatians 2:11).

With regard to the New Testament debate about Paul's apostolate to the Gentiles (ref. his letter to the Galatians), it may cause surprise to find the universal perspective of God's offer of salvation already present in the Old Testament. Abraham received, to be sure, a special mission as an individual. Yet from the very beginning of his vocation he did not stand for himself alone: "I will make of you a great nation, and I will bless you; I will make your name great, so that you will be a blessing. . . . All the communities of the earth shall find blessing in you" (Gn. 12:2-3). What is fundamental in this election of Abraham remains obscure: whether it is the choice of an individual for a universal mission or the blessing of all those whose instrument he was. The bond that united Moses with the Chosen People is similarly indissoluble. God, who wanted to destroy them (Ex. 32:10), allows the people of Israel to survive because Moses pleaded with him to do so (Ex. 32:11-14). Lastly, Jacob-Israel must also be understood as part of this people. For a whole night he wrestled with God and was disabled by him, but he also took away God's blessing from the encounter—not for himself alone, but also for his descendants (Gn. 32:25 ff.).

Mission

The vocation of individuals cannot be separated from their incorporation in the community and its mission. The people of God need to be assembled. Their mission to other peoples also remains constant. God's covenant with Noah involved the whole of creation. Even God's covenant with Abraham, which at first seems not to have included the totality of peoples, was soon extended and became universal in scope. At least by the time of the mission of the Servant of Yahweh the whole of humanity was comprised in it (Is. 42:6; 49:6).

In the key figures of the New Testament the need for a mission "to the ends of the earth" (Ac. 1:8) becomes unmistakable. The central personalities of the Gospels repeatedly testify to the universal scope of evangelization. Peter is placed as the rock of a church which is valid for the whole world and which is valid for all time. Paul knows that the Good News is for everyone and is to be denied to none of the uncircumcised. John—so closely linked to Jesus and Peter—stresses that love for all our brothers is the very touchstone for the sincerity of the love of God. Lastly, Mary, the utterly unique New Testament figure, is given by the Lord as New Testament mother to all the living, and the image of the universal church is enshrined in her virginal fruitfulness.

It follows from all this that the ecclesial community must always show a concern for those who do not yet belong to it. By the will of its founder, its nature consists in mission. The Christian community does not tolerate self-sufficiency or self-isolation. The phobia of entering into contact with others is inimical to it. The ghetto is its anti-model. Nor is it formed or defined by types of people, ethnic or otherwise, or by sexual allegiances. It is characterized not only by togetherness (a being-with-each-other): for Christ enables it to forge a redemptive reciprocity (a being-for-each-other). This is not as if Christians could "realize such a reciprocity on the same level as Christ, but because of the fact that they possess it in principle as the fruit of the unique 'being-for-all' of Christ on the cross."[12] The communion of saints thus grows by the mysterious force of this being-for-each-other in prayer, in substitution, in expiatory suffering. For this reason it is said that "the church, in Christ, is in the nature of sacrament—a sign and instrument, that is, of communion with God and of unity among all men" (*Lumen Gentium*, 1).

Universality

If the church's mission is addressed to humanity as a whole and the universal creation, then each community within it makes a claim to catholicity, and by doing so stands in absolute antithesis to the sects. Sects and spiritual movements are mutually exclusive, even if the latter are sometimes calumniated as sectarian.

There exists, indeed, from a sociological viewpoint, a similarity between both these forms of community, just as a similarity also exists between sects and religious orders.[13] This similarity provides in the first instance an opportunity for pastoral care. At any rate, this is how it is seen in a progress report published as a joint document by various offices of the Roman Curia in 1986.[14] The text summarizes a series of reports compiled by various regional and national bishops' conferences in response to a questionnaire sent out by the Secretariat for Christian Unity. It is not our present intention to review the contents of this document, which was motivated by the concerns raised by the significant growth and spread of the sects. However, it should at least be pointed out that some motivations—plausible in themselves—for the defection of Catholics to the sects equally provide a justification for the Catholic renewal movements from an unexpected quarter. This includes, for instance, the need for community felt by contemporary man and the various aspirations by which he is animated: for the meaning and wholeness of life; for cultural identity and also transcendence; for spiritual leadership; for participation and collaboration. The document in question then sums up as follows: "Almost all the responses [i.e., the replies received from the regional and national bishops' conferences] appeal for a rethinking (at least in many local situations) of the traditional 'parish community system'; a search for community patterns which will be more fraternal, more 'to the measure of man,' more adapted to people's life situations; more 'basic ecclesial communities'; caring communities of lively faith, love (warmth, acceptance, understanding, reconciliation, fellowship) and hope; celebrating communities; praying communities; missionary communities; outgoing and witnessing; communities open to and supporting people who have special problems: the divorced and 'remarried,' the marginalized" (3.1).

On the other hand, we cannot fail to notice the differences between spiritual movements and sects. The first such difference may be grasped at the sociological level. In the religious orders and renewal movements the turning away or withdrawal from the larger grouping of the church is never total and has no definitive character. The members of such orders and movements withdraw from the larger grouping for no other reason than to prepare for an eventual return to it. The backward progression is, so to say, aimed at ensuring that the run-up is longer and the resulting jump higher. While the sects reject, indeed despise, the established church, the spiritual movements gather their forces in "exodus" in order to transform the church by the spirit of the gospel.

Even more important, however, is the theological ground for the difference between spiritual movements and sects, as has already been mentioned: namely, the universal relevance of the message of Christ. Although he lived in a particular historical period and in a limited geographical area, Christ addressed himself to the men and women of all times and all places. By contrast, the sects absolutize the message and life-style of a particular phase in the development of Christianity. This phase then becomes normative. It is thus either extremely otherworldly or extremely historical. Sects tend to coalesce round a corresponding conception of community and to place themselves in irreconcilable opposition to current life. Any attempt at rapprochement, at an opening to the outside world, is branded as sacrilegious conformity. Those who remain "outside" are regarded only with contempt, or even with the conviction that they are heading for eternal damnation. Lastly, the sects refuse to recognize the Christ who continues to live in the church through history. The relation, full of tension but necessary, between church and world is unilaterally rejected in favor of their own community of faith.

Light

In antithesis to the sects, the church and each individual community within it are called to devote themselves to man and to everything that concerns him. "Man in the full truth of his existence of his personal being and also of his community and social being—in the sphere of his own family, in the sphere of society and very diverse contexts, in the sphere of his own nation or people . . . and in the sphere of the whole of mankind—this man is the primary route that the church must travel in fulfilling her mission: he is the primary and fundamental way for the church, the way traced out by Christ himself" (*Redemptor Hominis*, 14).

In the fulfillment of this task, the response to the tension between the message of the faith and the secularized world cannot of course be reduced to a compromise—as if the Christian were an honest broker, whose job it is to mediate between the two sides. It is not man himself who is the measure of the just relation between nature and grace, between culture and Christianity, between church and world. Rather, it is his task to bear witness to Christ in the world. Nowhere in Holy Scripture is it said that the way of the lesser evil is to be chosen. On the contrary, the Christian is challenged to an unconditional acceptance of the faith, to the indivisible response of the faith. This holds good for the Christian in every situation of life, in every place which has been given him by God in accordance with his way of life and his destiny. Whether in marriage or celibacy, in work or in leisure, in politics or social commitment, never is it granted him to follow a spirit other than that of his being a Christian.

For it is Christ in whom all things are created. God has put everything "under his feet" and "subjected everything to him" (1 Cor. 15:25, 27). The believer cannot therefore recognize any law that is independent of Christ and that pledges him to the powers of the world. He consequently does not have the right "to dominate the worldly situation with purely worldly judgments and methods."[15]

The church thus poses to herself the task of proclaiming the definitive redemption to the world. The church does not exist for her own sake, but serves the goal of striving to ensure that all things are accomplished through Christ in God. It follows that the world mission of the church indubitably concerns all her members. The members of the church are not only called to act outside it as individuals in the world, for the duty of service to the world is attributed to a particular class, i.e., the laity, alone. The allocations to persons and communities are motivated by the actual circumstances and places presented by their historical situation and tasks. It may therefore happen "that particular positions and functions devolve upon individual classes within the world mission of the church as a whole." Yet these particular positions and functions must never make us forget that "the whole church is missionary, because the head, whose body she is, is the whole mission of the Father" (*op. cit.*, 280).

The Second Vatican Council and, in particular, the synod of bishops held in Rome on the mission of the laity (1987) have emphasized that the laity are not second-class members of the church. All members of the church have responsibility for the universal mission, albeit in different situations and in varying degrees. No one is excluded. Still less is serious listening to the word of God limited to determined ecclesial groups.

Paul leaves us in no doubt that all the members of the community of Philippi are called to the same battle to which he himself is called (Ph. 1:30), i.e., the battle for the gospel (1:27). In his letter to the Ephesians, indeed, the battle is presented as a joint one: each must put on God's armor to struggle against "the world rulers of this present darkness" (Ep. 6:12). The gospel is devoid of casuistical rules that attribute lesser or greater perfection of the experience of faith to laity or nonlaity, or give scope to the often seductive temptation to evade its claims. All the baptized are "called to be holy" (1 Cor. 1:2); all are "God's chosen ones, holy and beloved," equally loved by God (Col. 3:12). Striving after perfection is not the privilege of experts (Col. 4:12; Ph. 3:15), even if perfection always remains a goal and can never be claimed, with smug self-satisfaction, to have been achieved. The words that Paul said of himself apply to everyone: "It is not that I have already taken hold of it or have already attained perfect maturity, but I continue my pursuit" (Ph. 3:12).

The mission of the church in the world takes the form of a twofold movement. The church assimilates the world to herself, and continuously passes over herself to go into the world. Both activities are intrinsic to her. On the one hand, everything that has entered the church from the world should have a reflex action by passing beyond her limits and reacting to the world outside. On the other hand, the church cannot expend herself exclusively in worldly service, for instance in an exclusive concern for peace and human well-being. Then the world would no longer be brought what it is incapable of obtaining by its own means—its redemption. "In a first movement the church must be really herself and increasingly become so in the assimilation of the world, to be able, in a second movement, to proclaim and give to the external world what is intrinsic to her" (*op. cit.*, 281). To illuminate, a source of light is needed, even if this always sheds light by departing from itself. The tree—to use another image—needs deeper roots, the greater its weight of foliage is. Whatever of the world is accepted and incorporated into the church cannot leave the world its worldliness. It is only insofar as it is transformed that worldliness can serve the mission of the church.

A look at the history of the church, which is in some way recapitulated in that of the renewal movements, provides confirmation of the rules outlined above. At the beginning of Christianity the aspect of separation is emphasized, just as the founders of renewal movements first withdrew from the world. Even when a universal mission is being prepared, the first step is that those doing so should distance themselves from the world. "Do not be yoked with those who are different, with unbelievers. . . . 'Come forth from them and be separate'" (2 Cor. 6:14,17). "Depart from her, my people, so as not to take part in her sins and receive a share in her plagues" (Rv. 18:4). "Do not conform yourself to this age" (Rm. 12:2).

The church took her time before becoming the community of saints, before introducing herself as yeast in the worldly state.

First came the Christian martyrs and holy virgins, the hermits and confessors. Only then did Christianity give form to architecture, the figurative arts and culture. The Christian churches are built in the spirit of the catacombs, and Christian policy only entered into view when great bishops "had rejected any tendency to compromise with worldly powers and raised the demand for the unbroken recognition of the church" (*op. cit.*, 283).

There can be no doubt about what task is imposed by the memory of this history. The acceptance of the world in the church has led in many places to a situation in which faith and kerygmatic capacity reveal phenomena of paralysis. David attempts to don the armor of Goliath, and the price he pays for doing so is immobility. The spiritual movements only maintain their versatility of movement if they reject as far as possible the apparatus and institutional aids of the church. What they must aim at is not an extensive but an intensive pastoral ministry. Only then does their mission to the world retain its force. Indeed, it is precisely in the church's divergence from the world that she acquires her meaning.

Laity

At this point the special contribution of the laity needs to be recalled briefly. The laity's mission derives from their "secular character," which is proper and particular to them. "By reason of their special vocation it belongs to the laity to seek the kingdom of God by engaging in temporal affairs and directing them according to God's will" (*Lumen Gentium*, 31). The evangelical counsels (traditionally identified as poverty, chastity and obedience), in no way addressed only to a reduced circle of ecclesiastics, will show the way.

The laity can in the first place make visible in the world the fact that the culture and property of a transient world order may be pressed into service of selfless Christian love. The gospel leaves no doubt that material, as well as intellectual, goods can represent antimoral forces that enslave people by their power. Paul, by contrast, repeatedly urges in his letters that they should be used as effective signs of brotherly love.[16]

This leads him, for instance, to hold up the communities in

Macedonia as an example: for they gave not only as much as they could afford, but far more, and quite spontaneously. They "begged us insistently for the favor of taking part in the service to the holy ones" (2 Cor. 8:3-4). By responding to the needs of others, they found their way to the merciful God, who rewards goodness. "The administration of this public service is not only supplying the needs of the holy ones but is also overflowing in many acts of thanksgiving to God" (9:12). Already in these early days the Apostles had created a special position in the church, that of the diaconate, so important is this ecclesial fire of love that is fed and nourished by the things of the world.

The second opportunity that the laity have of proclaiming the gospel to the world is that of making eros and sex transparent against the background of Christian *caritas*. Against those contemporaries who prohibited marriage and had therefore to be considered deceitful spirits and doctrines that come from the devils (1 Tm. 4:1-3), the Bible holds fast to the truth, "Let marriage be honored among all and the marriage bed be kept undefiled" (Heb. 13:4). The church is prefigured in the Word made flesh, in the virgin who became mother: nothing evil can therefore attach to the nuptial love ordained in the Incarnation. The Old Testament, for its part, celebrates human love with great freedom as an image of the affection of Yahweh himself for his people, for example in the Song of Songs. If the Word of God itself became flesh, and offered up its flesh for the life of the world, then it follows that flesh is not closed to the action of grace, that it is capable, on the contrary, of bearing the promise of salvation. The bond between man and woman is a sign of the definitive offering of the Redeemer on the cross: an offering by which his bride, the church, was made "without spot or wrinkle or any such thing" (Ep. 5:27). A Christian marriage, lived in a holy way, lights up the church to the world.

The laity, lastly, can provide the proof of the paradox that obedience leads to freedom. Given the automony of being able to choose, the freedom of a greater self-dedication may grow in someone who adapts himself to all-embracing obedience to the Lord of the church. Today there are many people, including members of the church herself, who are offended by this readiness to obey, if they do not dismiss it entirely. Still, this does not prevent them from enviously regarding someone who moves freely in obedience, because he is on the way to freedom in the

Spirit of God and is increasingly able to transcend the many forms of secular enslavement. "Even though he is able to determine his way anew each day, he still lives under the law of the 'once and for all' of Christ (Heb. 7:27; 9:12, etc.), by which he has been sealed by baptism. 'Again and again' (Heb. 9:25) the lay person must aim his freedom at sacrifice. This does not mean, though, that he is ultimately bound to renounce that freedom, any more than the man pledged to the evangelical counsels, just as he is not bound to renounce marriage and property" (*op. cit.*, 287).

The renewal movements are thus concerned not just with the proclamation of the gospel as a message of eternal salvation. The world and society are also, through history, the recipients of their words and actions. That this is so is especially because it is the laity who very frequently bear the responsibility for the renewal movements today and, on account of their "secular character," are exposed more strongly than the other members of the church to the tensions that affect the unity between the church and the world.

A large quantity of New Testament admonitions testify that the world's own force of gravity is opposed to all the forms that give scope to the evangelical counsels in the life of those who accept them. There are the almost threatening words addressed by Jesus against the rich (Mk. 10:23, etc.), or those contained in the Letter of James (5:1-4). There is the advice that Paul gives to Christians about living a married life that is pleasing to God (1 Cor. 7:1-16). There are the warnings about the abuse of freedom, which must find a middle way between Jewish legalism and pagan dissoluteness: "Do not submit again to the yoke of slavery" (Gal. 5:1), and: "For you were called for freedom, brothers. But do not use this freedom as an opportunity for the flesh; rather, serve one another through love" (Gal. 5:13). The world continuously seduces the elect to half-measures, so that James exhorts: "Draw near to God, and he will draw near to you. . . . purify your hearts, you of two minds" (4:8). All the members of the church are called to a greater maturity, to a growing willingness to accept the word of God, because "only the 'ever more' of renunciation and the following of Christ can also guarantee the 'ever more' of effectiveness, just as the length of the arrow's flight is proportioned to the tension of the bow" (*op. cit.*, 288).

3. Liturgy of the church

Revelation undoubtedly puts its finger on the temptation to which people of property, sexuality and power are prone. Still, it does not succumb to any form of hostility to the body or to the world, as if it wanted, in a Gnostic-Manichaean way, to separate the spirit from the body and devalue man's corporeal nature,[17] or to estrange him from the field of his life and his day-to-day action. It regards man not as a law unto himself, but as a being placed before God. It describes him where he encounters this God, where he stands before him, where he finds him and where God's presence is revealed to him. In other words, it sees man in the concrete circumstances of his life. It is there that man is chosen by God as his partner.

The way that God acts and reveals himself to man in the concrete realities of his life reached its culmination, and achieved its maximum depth, in Jesus Christ. God became man and subordinated himself to the laws of space and time. God's redemptive will was expressed in total incarnation. Jesus made his body the fulcrum of the divinization of man. In the light of the history of salvation, man can no longer trace his path to God along a purely spiritual way. Whoever lives and works does not react solely in spirit and mind, but also in the life of the senses. Thinking and willing have an impact on firmly delineated situations of life and on flesh-and-blood fellow men.

Undivided being

Spirit and senses are inextricably linked in man. This fact is evident in the life of Jesus himself. The Lord was born as an undivided and integral person. This is how he lived. This is how he suffered. This is how he died. This, too, is how he rose from the dead. Admittedly, a transformation took place between his death on the cross and his resurrection, but this does not mean that the body remained behind and that the spirit flew away. The Christ who died and the Christ who rose from the dead is the same.

Scripture therefore does not draw a distinction between the gift "of himself" for us and our sins, and the gift "of his soul" as redemption for the many, and the offering "of his body." During his earthly life Christ's soul lived in complete freedom; it did so "fully in his senses and affections. Jesus was

moved, indignant, angry, sorrowful, grieved to death; his corporeal life fully participated in all the mysteries of the soul,
right up to the end and even after his resurrection." In the biblical understanding, therefore, each human being—like Jesus
Christ himself—is not an amalgamation of two parts, the one
of the body, the other of the soul, which perhaps can have separate existences independently of each other. Man exists indi-
visibly in bodily and spiritual totality. "The corporeal being is
a body animated with a soul, which opens itself and organizes
itself as world and toward the world" (*op. cit.*, 371 ff.).

The pastoral content of man's corporeal-spiritual unity
and the impact that physical vitality has on the search for God
are expounded by Romano Guardini in his book *Die Sinne und
die religiose Erkenntnis.*[18] In Guardini's view, the cognitive capacity of the senses has become atrophied in the course of the
history of civilization. Instead of "seeing," man exercises his
mind by "observing." By the work of his intellect, he summarizes his observations into abstract truths. He is constantly a
prey to technology, which increasingly prevents him from let-
ting the great images of nature have their effect on him. "In
place of contemplated images, concepts have taken over; instead of incarnated images, apparatuses; instead of living
rhythms, segments of time." We speak of progress, but this, according to Guardini, is an absurdity. "In truth man becomes
sick in this way, for his inner being can only live from images"
(*op. cit.*, 63-65). Guardini refers to primitive peoples, among
whom empirical statements are embedded in religious life. By
the process of civilization "a disastrous reversal takes place by
which cultural acts such as knowledge, acting and creating are
decoupled from this context, and the religious act is turned
into a special performance" (*op. cit.*, 35). It is alienated from itself and loses any reference to life. Yet, on the contrary, the
senses could lead man to a living encounter with the creation.
Guardini has described this acceptance of the created environment by emphasizing the importance that the eye has in such a
cognitive process. The eye is *"par excellence* the man, in that it
can be struck by reality in the forms given to it by light" (*op.
cit.*, 22). The eye *sees* the life of the plants in the spectrum of
their colors, in the characteristics of their movements caused
by air and motion. It sees the life of the animals. In man it sees
the spirit in gestures, in expressions and in activities. In the
eye, as in the other senses, the world opens itself up to man.

These are not at all fictitious theses, removed from reality, and artificially thought up in the study. The philosopher of culture formulates, on the contrary, insights about man that are true for all men and that are, for some, concretely tangible in spectacular events, as they were, for instance, for Charles de Foucauld in his conversion.

On June 30, 1882, this 24-year-old French officer resigned his commission, and left for Morocco to conduct geographical, ethnological and linguistic research. He left behind him the life of a rake and an idler in the cavalry school of Saumur, and a liaison with Mimi, a girl who became his mistress in Evian. The Sahara exposed him to all the power of a bizarre and never-before-experienced world of nature, to all its physical arduousness and vivid impressions of the senses. The pristine uncorrupted creation overwhelmed him. The people who lived in it spoke to him a new language. He saw the Arabs who in the worship of their God prostrated themselves in the sand of the desert.

Three years later he wrote to his nephew Henri de Castries: "Islam has aroused in me a great transformation. . . . The sight of this faith, of these people who live in the constant presence of God, has made me understand something, something far greater and far truer than all the hustle and bustle of the world."[19] The experience of nature and the peoples assocated with it can thus become a healing experience for the man sick of civilization; he is mentally and spiritually cured. H. Laperrine, a colleague of Charles de Foucauld during his years as an officer, later reported: "This life in the midst of convinced believers delivered the coup de grace to Foucauld's skepticism. He admired the strength that all these Moroccans derived from their faith, both the fanatic and fatalistic Muslims and the Jews, who remain indissolubly bound to their religion in spite of centuries of persecution."[20]

Eye and ear, taste and feeling are able to apprehend God, and to know him. Even though rationalists and traditionalists are afraid of it, this approach of the senses to God is not dictated by mere enthusiasm. God's eternal power and glory are expressed in his works, the Apostle to the Gentiles assures us (Rm. 1:18 ff.). Throughout the history of revelation the presence and action of God have been perceived and understood by people in many forms. His "apparitions" sustain the message of both the Old and New Testaments. Yet, Guardini asks,

"What became of the epiphanic after the Lord returned to his Father"?[21] After his departure, what is it that strikes the senses of man, if he is no longer there to be seen? Have the senses perhaps become useless for a meeting with God? Guardini himself replied to these questions. The liturgy gives our senses the chance of serving as a bridge to God. Man creates symbols for himself in objects and gestures, and extends the sense he has of himself to them. In the liturgy he offers oblation, not with his mere hands, but in a bowl, a surface that is open to God above and holds itself out toward him. The clouds of incense reinforce the expression of ascension, which is embodied in the raised faces and hands of the prayer. The column of the candle, on whose tip the flame rises and consumes itself in burning, signifies the interior attitude of voluntary donation. The person who prays acts out his prayer: he kneels or sits, genuflects, clasps or joins his hands together, stretches his arms, beats his breast, embraces his brother or sister in the sign of peace. Thus man's bodily movement and action are in themselves pregnant with great meaning.

Yet the physical world, the world of things, acquires a new status when it is directly placed at the service of the sacrament. In water, in oil, in the signs of bread and wine we recognize, in faith, God's action, his presence. Whoever sees them is not an enthusiast (in the pejorative sense) or a miracle-seeker. What happens to him is "something entirely normal . . . 'normal,' of course, in the order of grace, in which remains that of the incarnation" (*op. cit.*, 55). "That the 'sign' is not only indicative but revelational is the free choice of the Lord in the liturgy" (*ibid.*, 59).

The acceptance of created things and human gestures makes the liturgy an act of fundamental affirmation. Man says yes to his Creator; he says yes to the creation. Affirmation is indeed the basic form of the Christian cult. Each prayer ends with an "Amen": a word signifying assent—"So be it!" The "Hallelujah," in turn, is an expression of thanksgiving for God's greatness and his offer of salvation to man. The eucharistic prayer is the epitome of the glorifying affirmation of God's salvific action in Christ, the praise of the Trinity, in which the celebrating community and each individual in it give their assent to the Lord's act of redemption and open themselves to it.

Things and people are created anew in the liturgy. It releases a space of participation that transcends the walls of the here and now. Celebrating means "exposing oneself to the presence of the deity" (Odo Casel). The day-to-day existential dimension is opened up, and things and people are transported. A breathing space is produced. Time stands still, and the community of celebrants is released from the constraints of everyday life. The Christian's great liturgical act is thus called "thanksgiving": the praise and glorification of God for his act of salvation in Jesus Christ, and, together with it, the affirmation of the world and of existence as a whole. *"C'est l'amour qui chante*—only the lover sings," quotes Josef Pieper in his essay *"Zustimmung zur Welt."*[22] Song here means not only poetry and music, but the grateful response for all the things that the Lord and Redeemer has bestowed on man in love.

Salvation in the sign

The community of believers lives from the liturgical celebration of God. Vatican II's *Constitution on the Sacred Liturgy* wrung from the council fathers—not without the opposition of some—the demanding affirmation: "The liturgy is the summit toward which the activity of the Church is directed; it is also the fount from which all her power flows" (*Sacrosanctum Concilium*, 10). This evaluation of the liturgy may seem acceptable if we look at what is delineated in the celebration of the sacraments; insofar as Baptism and the Eucharist, for instance, derive from and point to the redemptive death of Christ. However, clearly what is meant by the conciliar affirmation is not Christ's salvific action as such, it is the liturgical action itself that is defined as the summit and fundamental source of the church's activity. In other words, this amazing quality is attributed to what the faithful enact under the guise of signs.

This high evaluation can only be justified if the celebration of the liturgy is more than the turning of the faithful to God. Only if it is God himself who acts in the midst of his community can it make sense. Human activity thus becomes an opportunity for God's presence to be felt, and his action to transpire. To put the matter in the words of article 7 of the same document, "Christ is always present in his church, especially in her liturgical celebrations," so that, as Augustine says, when anybody baptizes it is really Christ himself who baptizes.[23] In the liturgical event, therefore, it is Christ's action that is revealed in the mystery. It penetrates man's sphere of life in veiled form. It reaches the celebrants at the very borders, as it were, of their cognitive capacity. Thus the celebration of the mystery of faith can become a moment of grace.

That God grants participation in salvation through the liturgy and that man can actually grasp this act of God are confirmed by St. Paul. Through his guidance to the Corinthians Paul draws a picture of a community in which a liturgy of great liveliness and variety is performed (1 Cor. 14). Prayer, the praise of God in song, the proclamation of the word of God and the celebration of the Lord's Supper as thanksgiving to the Father can all be recognized. Some verses also give an idea of the effects that the celebration has on those gathered together for it. The continuous building up of the community (vv. 3-5) derives from the liturgy. No believer can ever be satisfied with the level he has reached of dedication to God's will and disinterested love.

In other passages the Apostle Paul deals with the fruits that the liturgical celebration may produce in unbelievers and the uninitiated (vv. 16, 22-24). Paul clearly attributes a missionary character to the liturgical action, too. The logic and structure of the whole chapter prove indeed that it was just these thoughts that the Apostle wanted to communicate. The argument proceeds to its conclusion in its culminating verse: "But if everone is prophesying, and an unbeliever or uninstructed person should come in, he will be convinced by everyone and judged by everyone, and the secrets of his heart will be disclosed, and so he will fall down and worship God, declaring, 'God is really in your midst'" (v. 25).

Therefore, there is no doubt that, in its texts, in its proclamation and in its sacred action, the liturgy transmits a knowledge of the faith. Theology has always affirmed that the mode of prayer provides the foundation to the mode of belief (*lex orandi—lex credendi*). Beyond this, however, the celebration of the liturgy releases certain elements of knowledge about God and his salvific actions in man that evidently move the human will more strongly to seek the direct and personal confrontation with this God. This confrontation may result in the act of self-knowledge and self-giving.

In the celebration of the liturgy, the word of God reaches man's inner ear more effectively and more forcefully. In the praying congregation it proclaims, reveals and converts. The belief in the presence of the Lord is the light that brings to light the works of man (Jn. 3:20). What was hidden is revealed: error, sin. God's love for and appeal to unbelievers are brought to light. Darkness and blind superficiality are expelled. The consequence? Man prostrates himself. Someone is won for the adoration of God. The meeting with the God who reveals himself forces us to bend our knees. It is he himself who is active in this event. It is he who compels out into the light the heart that sought to hide itself. It is he who dispels man's illusion of being an equal partner of God, and places before his eyes the vision of God's majesty instead. Man is humbled; he bows his head; he falls to his knees. To describe this act of adoration, Paul adopted the Greek word *"proskynein,"* which also means "entering God's special protection."

This inward emotion is one that man cannot keep to himself. It forces him to shout it out loud, to share it with others. However, in so doing he does not speak of himself. Nor does he speak of what God has worked inside him. Rather, he confesses God's presence in the liturgy of the community. He looks away from himself; only God and his worship are of interest to him. His glory must be proclaimed, and that is also the glory of the community: "God is among you indeed!"

The few New Testament references to the forms of liturgical service in the early church enable us at least to intuit their infectious movement. They lead to the conclusion that the everyday liturgy in our own time, which is detectable behind the momentum of the early Christian practice, is lagging behind. Undoubtedly the founding phase of Christianity should also provide the basic criterion, or at least give guidelines, for the liturgy today. Even if the intervention of God's grace can never be compelled, nor its influence on the spiritual capabilities of man calculated, no one can doubt that the presuppositions for a step toward the deepening of faith can be either an obstacle or an aid. That was why the Apostle Paul gave his instructions to the Corinthians.

Paul Claudel

Even in our own day, men and women in search of God experience the motive force of the liturgy. They testify to the fact that meaningful divine services and persuasive liturgical forms can reach and move the soul. This experience was made by the French poet Paul Claudel. While still a young man he had lost his faith and lived, as he put it, in "a state of despair."[24] At the same time he felt a great spiritual hunger inside himself. On Christmas Day, 1886, he happened to enter the Cathedral of Notre Dame in Paris and joined the congregation at Mass—more to observe than to pray, as he confesses. The solemn high Mass afforded him "a mild degree of pleasure." Then in the afternoon he returned to the cathedral and attended Vespers. In his account of his conversion, Claudel provides the precise details of the moment and place in the church in which his life was decisively changed: "The choirboys were singing what I later discovered to be the Magnificat. I was standing in the midst of the crowd, near the second pillar by the entrance to the choir, to the right, on the side of the sacristy. And it was there that the event took place that was to dominate my whole life. In an instant my heart was touched, and I believed."

Certainly the step toward faith is above all an event of grace. Nonetheless, the senses remain the doors to the soul. Already the scholastic doctrine of cognition in the Middle Ages affirmed that nothing occurs in the intellect without first passing through the senses.[25]

It follows that man can only be led to take a decision by what penetrates his mind through the senses. That is why faith can be instilled, and conversion take place, by what he has heard—through the ears through which the message of salvation is brought to man (Rm. 10:14). Apart from the ear, though, the other senses also play their part. The celebration of the liturgy heightens them and makes them responsive to the meeting with God. It was the senses that made Claudel conscious of the worshiping congregation in the midst of which he was standing; of the choral singing and the music, which the aesthetic sensibility of the church has created over the centuries; of the sacred spectacle of the liturgical action, its ministers, its gestures, its rites, its colors, its light and darkness. Last but not least, it made him aware of the space of the Gothic cathedral itself in which he was standing, a building of awe-inspiring beauty, in which the artistic sense of generations and generations and the will to the adoration of God have assumed concrete embodiment in stone. It is certainly not by accident that, in the course of his brief account, Claudel specifies no less than three times the exact place where he was standing.

Franz Rosenzweig

Another witness in our century to the faith experienced as the spiritual effect that liturgical celebration can have on its participants is Franz Rosenzweig (d. 1929). He is considered one of the most significant thinkers of Judaism and, together with Martin Buber, produced an exemplary translation of the Old Testament into German.[26]

In 1913 it seemed to Rosenzweig that the moment had come to be baptized and enter the Evangelical Church. He wanted to do so, however, not as a pagan but as a Jew, and so chose the way that leads to Christianity through Judaism, just as, in his opinion, the founders of Christianity themselves had done. He therefore sought a new relationship with the faith of his childhood from which he had become estranged. He later wrote to R. Ehrenburg: "I explained I could only cross over to Christianity as a Jew, not through the intermediate state of paganism."[27] He therefore wished to participate in the Jewish liturgical feast of Yom Kippur, the Day of Atonement.

This is one of the most important feasts in the Jewish religious calendar. Its liturgy begins on the previous evening. It is opened by the prayer of "All Vows" that is recited in tones of lamentation to pray for release from all erroneous or forgotten vows. All guilt, including that against fellow believers, must first be erased. This is followed by the remission of the sins that man has before God.

Yom Kippur is celebrated by a daylong fast. The liturgy in the synagogue comprises scriptural readings which heighten the believer's obligations to his neighbor: "releasing those bound unjustly, . . . breaking every yoke; Sharing your bread with the hungry, sheltering the oppressed and the homeless" (Is. 58:6-7). Psalms and hymns lift the gaze of the community toward God. The liturgical rites make present in each synagogue the service performed in the Temple of Jerusalem by the high priest, who alone on that day is permitted to pronounce the inexpressible name of God, Yahweh, "who is close to those who invoke him." Like the high priest, who enters the Holy of Holies in white vestments, all the worshipers are dressed with the white *kittel* (or prayer shawl).

This dress has an additional meaning in the liturgy. It recalls the shroud that will be worn on the day of death. The worshiper thus feels himself to be a poor man in front of the

Almighty, the Universal Judge. Although he finds himself in the circle of his fellow believers, he recognizes that he stands alone in his absolute, inescapable responsibility which he alone must bear. Without any outside help, he stands before his God.

Before the doors are shut just before sunset, the worshipers once again supplicate Yahweh that they be allowed to cross over the threshold of God's door, so as to live eternity within the confines of time. Then, with great solemnity, the congregation proclaims aloud its profession of faith: "Hear, O Israel! The Lord is our God, the Lord alone!" (Dt. 6:4), followed by the declaration, "The Lord is God: the Lord of love. He alone is God." After this profession of faith, the ram's horn is blown, and the long day draws to an end.

After participating in the Yom Kippur liturgy, Franz Rosenzweig was a different man. Admittedly, he never thereafter spoke of the importance and the consequences of this event. Indeed, no written account of the effect on him of that day is extant. Nonetheless, his decisions and subsequent observations enforce the conclusion that his participation in the liturgy induced in him a fundamental change of heart. During a lecture he gave years later in the Free Jewish Academy in Frankfurt, he said, for example: "Whoever has once celebrated Yom Kippur knows that it is more than a mere personal rapture (though this can play a part) or the recognition in symbolic form of a reality like that of the Jewish people (though this too may play a part); it is a witness of the reality of God, which cannot be contradicted" (XIX ff.). In his main work, *Star of Redemption*, he describes how on the Day of Atonement the Jew meets his God: "Man is utterly alone on the day of his death, when he is dressed in his shroud, and in the prayers of these days (the Days of Awe culminating in the Day of Atonement) he is also alone. . . . he confronts the eyes of his Judge in utter loneliness, as if he were dead in the midst of life. . . . His soul stands, without help or protection, before him. In that moment God lets himself be touched by the supplicating throng of worshipers and gives man part of his eternal life" (XX).

It would certainly be a misunderstanding of Judaism to suppose that its liturgy is celebrated on behalf of man. It is beyond question that this religion in particular celebrates, in the feasts of the faithful, its God and Savior. The worship of

Yahweh has no subsidiary or auxiliary purpose. The faith's central formula, indeed, even an accurate description of its religious institutions in general, is: "for Yahweh." This goes for the feast of pilgrimage, the Passover, and for the Sabbath itself.[28]

The Jew is profoundly penetrated by the conviction that God has an exclusive right over man, over his time and over his worship.

Yet the worship that is due to Yahweh is at the same time the means of obtaining grace from him. The commemorative thanksgiving for his great deeds becomes for the worshiper a renewed sign of the love and redemption of the Lord and Savior. Divine service is thus, in essence, an act of commemoration or remembrance, in which Yahweh and Israel may reciprocate as its protagonists. Both remember each other and recall to themselves the past, which in this way becomes present. Language and liturgical action play a powerful part in this. The *Mishna* treatise on the feast of Passover thus declares: "In each generation a man is pledged to consider himself as if he had fled out of Egypt, for it is written: 'On that day you shall tell your son: "For the sake of what the Lord did for me, when I came out of Egypt."' We are therefore bound to thank, praise, glorify, exalt, adore, bless, magnify and pay homage to him who performed these wonders for our forefathers and for us all."[29]

Paul Claudel and Franz Rosenzweig confirmed, each in his own way, that the liturgy is the privileged place for an effective apostolate. Anyone who reflects on the renewal of the church and the impulses that are necessary today for evangelization cannot pass over the liturgical act in silence. He should also consider the special attention that the renewal movements devote to it. Some of the latter's experiences are indeed well suited to achieve the further progress of the postconciliar process of liturgical deepening.[30] John Paul II's apostolic letter *Vicesimus Quintus Annus*, published on the occasion of the 25th anniversary of Vatican II's *Constitution on the Sacred Liturgy*, explicitly remarks on the liturgy's missionary character. The act of worshiping God commits the church to the mission of spreading the gospel in the world (no. 9).

Reference points for today

Only a few brief remarks can be made here about what in the liturgy deserves particular attention today. Their point of departure is the conviction that the period of pronounced rationality, to which Guardini has already drawn attention, is still far from behind us. Indeed, it has strongly influenced the implementation of liturgical reform during the postconciliar period. Typical of this mentality is a statement made by Hirzenberger in 1969. Apropros of the liturgical reform, he called for "exact historical-critical knowledge" with a view to the analysis of the current forms. Its findings should then be confronted "with the original" forms, so as to "ascertain the conflicting, the outmoded and the contradictory, and so distance it as dangerous and deviant."[31] The reform of the liturgy should be placed, in other words, under the dictates of the pure intellect. In the interpretation of Guardini and Balthasar, on the contrary, the liturgical form should today be consciously filled instead with anthropological and theological contents, though without abandoning the grounds of rationality to seek refuge in some kind of mystical penumbra. The following goals should point in the right direction.

Being in tune with the times. Social tensions are a part of human reality. Ecology and peace form part of our vital concerns, and therefore must also find a place in the liturgy. Yet social reality is not the only, nor is it the most important, reference point for the liturgy. Divine service should not be exploited by turning it into a programmatic assembly which identifies itself, say, with the goals of moral rearmament, or even transforms itself into a forum for a particular protest group.

After the raising of major sociopolitical questions during the 1960s and 1970s, we have all in the meantime learned something. Psychology has drawn our attention loudly and clearly to the psychic and spiritual structures of man. We have rediscovered that man cannot live without images. The wisdom of myths and fables has occupied the attention of anthropologists in the interpretation of human existence. A new and enhanced value is now attached to nature, and increased concern shown for its protection.

All this teaches the church's pastoral ministry that the *cosmic* dimension of human existence must be borne in mind.

New Age is a telling example of the change in sensibility that has taken place.

The close link with concrete life. The joys and sorrows of celebrating Christians need their place in the liturgy. The communal and individual experience of life and of faith must be given an outlet in divine service. For in this way it, too, can assimilate the cognitive progress given to the individual and the community about the way to God. Knowledge about God cannot remain dead knowledge, against which the letter of James warned.[32] Faith, on the contrary, is expressed not in facts, but in praise and thanksgiving before God. In this way the liturgical celebration is also protected from a fatal isolation. Witness to Christ in daily life and the service to the poor, to our neighbor "at the door," make the liturgy more truthful. *Leiturgia* continues to refer to *martyria* and *diakonia*. If the Christian holds these three things in small repute, his Christian being becomes atrophied. This connection of the liturgy with daily life needs especially to be observed in those local churches in whose catechumenate for adults and seminaries an academic system has developed which is merely occupied with the cognitive dimension of faith. The liturgical celebration ought to be a kind of culminating point of an "examination of conscience": in every act of worship for each individual, does not the hustle and bustle of its performance too often hinder every form of contemplation? On occasion is this not also true for the individual in front of the community? This examination of conscience can be understood as "decodification of the data [of daily life] in the light of the gospel."[33]

In the church. This close contact of the liturgy with daily life must not, however, interfere with fidelity to the church's prescribed forms. There is sufficient scope for freedom, and it is there to be used. Whoever, by contrast, ignores parts of the liturgy or adds rites that go beyond the prescribed norms, whoever substitutes profane texts for readings from Holy Scripture, that person is guilty of abuses which it is up to the bishops to root out. Initiatives of this sort, as John Paul II declares in his apostolic letter *Vicesimus Quintus Annus,* "far from being linked with the liturgical reform . . . , are in direct contradiction to it, disfigure it and deprive the Christian people of the genuine treasures of the liturgy of the church" (no. 13).

The liturgy always remains the liturgy of the universal church. "Liturgical services are not private functions but are celebrations of the church" (*Constitution on the Sacred Liturgy,* no. 26). Anyone who celebrates the liturgy outside the bond of unity with the church inflicts grievous wounds on the church, even if the celebration is canonically valid.

As people endowed with senses. The signs offered by the

liturgy must be readable. It is not enough to perform the rite correctly and allow all the prescribed words to be heard in a more or less comprehensible way. Major importance attaches to everything that the senses apprehend during it. The objects used in the rite must speak by themselves. It is not a bare minimum, but a certain prodigality of signs that speaks to the senses of the celebrants. Sight, taste, smell and touch can help the faithful to open themselves to the Lord under the forms of bread and wine, to believe the anointing of the Spirit present in the perfume of the chrism. Gestures, vestments and liturgical furnishings are there to be seen. In his liturgical catecheses, St. Ambrose, bishop of Milan, continually refers to what the eyes of the body see.[34]

The comment of an indubitably impartial theologian on the preconciliar liturgy of the Catholic Church should give us pause for thought, even in our own day: "Whereas the Protestant parish service, in its intellectual sobriety and ethical severity, has difficulty in releasing vital forces of individual piety in the broad masses of the average faithful, the liturgy of the Catholic Mass has, in . . . its wealth of sensual and aesthetic stimuli, for centuries been the springboard of mystical prayer and contemplation. It is beyond doubt that in the Catholic sacramental liturgy . . . people pray more, and with greater inwardness, than in the Protestant spoken service."[35]

For the will of God. In one of his books, the Swiss hagiographer Walter Nigg has occasion to speak of St. Teresa of Avila's complaint about how many bad priests there were. Repeatedly in her *Autobiography* and in her letters she mentions this burden that lies on her soul. The author asks himself what exactly this saint meant by a bad priest: benefice-seekers, careerists eager for honors? Then Walter Nigg gives the answer himself: "Perhaps, above all, however, those priests who—to use an expression of Holderlin—'pursue the divine as if it were a trade,' natures inwardly indifferent, men without spirituality."[36]

To pursue the divine as if it were a trade. The atmosphere of the liturgy depends, more markedly than all pastoral care, on the person who officiates it. God will hardly be found in it if the person officiating it pursues the divine as if it were a trade. He and all celebants are reminded by the *Constitution on the Liturgy* of the sentence from the Rule of St. Benedict: "Standing before God we sing the psalms so that our mind may concur with our voice."[37]

4. On the way to abundant life (Jn. 10:10)

Even though the impetus for spiritual movements has, both in the past and in the present, come very frequently from lay people, the ordained ministers of the church have an important, and in the long term unrelinquishable, role to play in them.

Yet a serious obstacle to the growth and diffusion of these movements lies precisely in this fact. The great burden of work on the pastors of souls has as its consequence that they are reluctant to assume any additional duties. The clergy in the parishes are disinclined to get involved, since they consider themselves already overburdened, and with the eyes of the bishops on them. In other respects frictions are only to be expected; conflicts and tensions will inevitably place curbs on programed pastoral work. Pastoral commitments are multiplied, since each group demands its right. Only a naive person still has the courage to apply to his situation such proverbs as "the more the merrier" or *variatio delectat*.

No one, however, should consider the shortage of priests as a pretext for the rejection of new initiatives. Pastors are lacking in many dioceses. Their absence has only increased the forces employed in the administrative sector. These need to be relieved. Yet they too are pressing for a standardization which would subordinate the pastoral ministry as far as possible to the bureaucratic process. Already bureacracy has entered the pastoral sector of the formulation of standardized programs. Special measures of every kind only cause unnecessary effort.

Yet there is also something else that needs to be borne in mind. All pastoral effort does not have its sense in itself. A well-ordered, efficient system of operation is no doubt desirable, but it can never be allowed to become a purpose in itself. All structures and services of the church have a relative importance—in other words, they are not ends in themselves, but are aimed at opening the working of the Spirit of God to the believer. They are subordinated to the Spirit's illumination and strengthening of the baptized.

Opportunities for variety

Vatican II's *Dogmatic Constitution on Divine Revelation, Dei Verbum,* specifies the sanctification of man by means of the Spirit of God as the goal of the whole reality of the church. "It is clear, therefore, that, in the supremely wise arrangement of

God, sacred Tradition, sacred Scripture and the Magisterium of the Church are so connected and associated that one of them cannot stand without the others. Working together, each in its own way under the action of the one Holy Spirit, they all contribute effectively to the salvation of souls" (no. 10). The Holy Spirit is cited no less than 33 times in this document. It is in the Spirit that sacred Scripture is inspired; it is in the Spirit that it is further interpreted through all time in doctrine, in life and in culture, so that the apostolic tradition, strengthened by the Spirit, may advance to new insights. Help in doing so is provided not only by the "spiritual realities" that the faithful experience, but also by "the sure charism of truth" bequeathed by apostolic succession to the episcopate, whose task it is, "enlightened by the Spirit of truth, [to] faithfully preserve, expound and spread it abroad by their preaching" (nos. 8-9).

If then the word of God and the ministry of the church are so closely interrelated with the action of the Spirit on man, how much more so must the modes of pastoral practice, whether traditional or modern, be subordinated to this end. The question therefore cannot be avoided, whether even much-loved pastoral styles and forms of apostolate need to be replaced, since they serve but little, in human judgment, for the transmission of the Spirit. This question must be posed in response to a world and society undergoing rapid change, even though there will be those who will peremptorily dismiss it with the assertion that they are against change and remain loyal to the church's tradition, and that for them the history of the church and its pastoral institutions are sacrosanct. No one can simply equate the immutability of the heritage of the faith with the most reliable forces and modes of pastoral service.

Forms of piety are variable. Times and places, history and culture, the individual circumstances of life of those who promote them and their individual characteristics—all have an effect on them and lead to differentiations. This is a conclusion that follows from the inner logic of spirituality itself.[38] Spirituality is the subjective side of dogmatics. It is for its initiators a kindling and instantaneous experience of divine revelation. Each spiritual project, and hence the original impulse of each spiritual movement, begins with a person who experiences "an interior revolution deriving from a basic encounter of the believer with revelation." This individual call can enable someone to grasp how "God should, or should not, be thought about" (*op. cit.*, 230). In the case of the founder of a movement, it often means grasping in the experience of revelation a clearly delineated and comprehensible content—almost a keyword, which epitomizes the founder's call and delineates the perspective of the pastoral impulse as a whole, a "newly opened window" to enable us "to look into the heart of the gospel."[39] Instantaneous experiences of this kind may reduce the gospel, but they also help to define and promote it. The character of revelation changes when a person undergoes such an inner revolution and receives the call. It acquires a dynamic dimension. An objectively valid doctrine becomes the impetus for conduct and action. Theory provokes decision, and this in turn acts as an irresistible impulse to action. The variety of the spiritual movements is thus the other side of the coin from their often admired dynamism. It is the price to be paid for ensuring that the word of God remains ever young, and ever dynamic, in the history of mankind.

However, does not the ability to choose among evangelical truths arouse suspicion of heresy?

It is not the numerical total of the individually revealed truths which is the gauge of the genuineness and vitality of our faith, however important the comprehensive theological elucidation of revelation as a whole may be. What matters for the individual is rather the *ever deeper* penetration of the mystery. It is this which leads to the center of the faith, and which can recover for us a vision of its unity.

It is "the transition from the arduous multiplicity of the word to the gathering of silence." The intellect has tasted the content of the faith; it has defined its contours, verified its presuppositions, developed its consequences. Then faith irradiates the soul, "and the more it does so, the more simple it makes the soul, and hence the more simple it makes itself, until it becomes inexpressible." St. Ambrose described this process as follows: "The sign of God is the simplicity of the faith." That this occurs is not the result of indolence or inertia. It is not narrowness nor the striving after abstraction that drives the interior human being. Simplicity "gives away nothing that the word has obtained, but it interiorizes everything and so brings it to unity."[40]

Augustine prays: "Deliver me, O God, from the multitude of words with which I am inwardly afflicted in my soul. It is wretched in your sight, and takes refuge in your mercy. For I am not silent in my thoughts, even when I am silent in my words. . . . A certain wise man, when he spoke of you in his book [Ecclesiasticus], declared: 'We say many things and fall short; and the sum of our words is, he is all' (Sir. 43:29). But when we shall come to you, these 'many things' which we say 'and fall short' shall cease; and you as One shall remain, you who are all in all (1 Cor. 15:28); and without ceasing we shall say one thing, praising you with one voice, we who have also been made one in you. O Lord, the one God, God the Trinity."[41]

Those who complain about the multiplicity of the new spiritual impulses in the church today should ponder for a moment the history of revelation.[42] According to the witness of Scripture itself, God proclaimed and worked his salvation in ever new movements and ever changing persons. The spirituality of the exodus from Egypt was fundamentally different from that experienced by the people of Yahweh during their 40 years in the wilderness. Equally, the way that service before God was understood during the period of the judges is different from that in the time of the kings. While the wisdom books evidently take account of sound common sense, the prophets strenuously urge the rights due to God from his people. The revelation of God in the Old Testament not only presents different aspects of the same truths, "but also and at the same time essentially . . . [present] a new mode of divine revelation, adapted to the changing situation, but at the same time codetermined in a decisive way by this same situation. It is precisely for this reason that the people of God so often refused to obey."

This Old Testament conception is made even more tangible in Jesus Christ. Despite overall similarity in orientation, he created something unmistakably different in the mission entrusted to each of his chosen disciples. "Peter and John, Paul and James, Martha and Mary of Bethany, Mary Magdalen, Lazarus, the woman of Samaria: each of them unique and whole, each of them embodying unique realities of encounter, but realities in each of which the indivisible and whole Jesus is revealed" (*op. cit.*, 232).

It is noteworthy that the tradition has never conflicted with the multiplicity of spiritual standpoints and contents. Already Origen acknowledged the right, indeed the need, for diversity of perspectives in the church, "so that the plenitude of the one *Logos* may develop itself within her in human forms" (*ibid.*, 233). Other Fathers of the church, while expressing their concern for the unity of the church, have accorded high value to the individuality of the great masters, and regarded it as exemplary.

Yves de Montcheuil, a classic name in French 20th-century theology, writes "that nothing is more conflicting with true Christian unity than the impetus to unification. The latter always consists in the attempt to proclaim the universal validity of an individual form, and to imprison life in one of its forms of expression."[43] In the last analysis, therefore, it is not the sociological integration of a spiritual impulse with the structure of the church that provides the proof of the phenomenon's ecclesiality. The adaptation of the new to the existing structure may seem laudable and desirable, but it is not the criterion by which its quality can be assessed. That criterion consists exclusively in the fruits it bears, namely, that members of the church be led, in the framework of ecclesial tradition and doctrine, to a greater dedication in faith, and so to the witness of love before their local community.

New spiritual impulses disturb. This affirmation is abundantly confirmed by history; it is also psychologically persuasive. Man is vulnerable in his way of living the faith. An unusual and alien style of presenting the faith may upset. It may also challenge. In persons of delicate sensibility the question is posed involuntarily. Is the other person's way of expressing his Christianity more suited to the content of the faith? Is it more right? Perhaps I, too, need to do likewise.

This uncertainty is well founded. For a religious truth is made visible in the form in which it is actually expressed. Conversely, the individual believer can have no proof of its certainty other than by believing it. A new way of believing must therefore irritate. Sometimes it may provoke an unconsidered reaction; calling into question my way of believing seems to threaten the truth of my faith as such. The result is that I place myself on the defensive by a show of intolerance toward what is unusual. Moreover, if I am socially confirmed in my own way, then I will have certainty not only about the style of my faith but also about its content.

Consequently, hitherto unknown spiritual impulses tend to be rejected not only by virtue of a pastoral practice aimed at reinforcing harmony and comprehensibility, but also, and no less sharply, on the basis of psychic anxieties. Even so, these anxieties can hardly pronounce on the value and meaning of spiritual action. That we must not simply acquiesce in the spontaneous psychological contagion provoked by the threat to the habitual has already been shown by the impressive fruits of the new spiritual impulses of the past. Those who consult the empirical sciences will find other arguments, besides. Despite the limited scope of the present book, it is right that at least something should be said of these arguments, in order to obtain further corroboration of the need for diversity and multiplicity of forms and associations within the church.

Sociological confirmations

For sociology,[44] so-called premodern society can be distinguished by the fact that it has a unified upper class. This latter creates communication among all the persons responsible for political decisions, for jurisprudence and for military and religious leadership. Artists and the nobility belong to it. This upper class is also inseparably linked with the principle of locality. Those who work alongside one another in the same place are naturally brought into association. It is also characterized by a corporate ethos and an ideologically homogeneous life-style.

The overwhelming proportion of citizens in premodern society are excluded from the upper class. They are not only kept outside it, but are even denied any opportunity of communicating with those who are privileged by it.

In modern society independent subsystems are developed with various functions. Social institutions—the government and judiciary, the army and religious communities, health care, education and commerce—develop their own independence in relation to the specific purposes for which they are designed. The "art of power" of the upper class is differentiated. It is no longer exclusively confined to it, and begins to be disseminated to other groups. This development occurs *pari passu* with the birth of new ideas. In principle they are accessible to all those interested. New spaces of communication thus originate.

Modern society originated in Europe in the 18th and 19th centuries. Its motive force is functional differentiation. As Tenbruck rightly points out, differentiation is "considered the unique characteristic of the modern society that emerged from Europe." Thus, what at first appears as the decomposition of society is in reality of benefit to its invigoration and network of relations.

In a sociological study on modernization, socialization, group formation and associational life, F.H. Tenbruck and W.A. Ruopp subject to examination the forces which have generated this social differentiation and improvement of communication among people.[45] They enunciate a number of theses, which can for purposes of our present argument be briefly summarized as follows.

1. The associational movement of the 19th century released, through the formation of new social groups, those dynamic forces which progressively fostered the relationships among them. Association thus came to mean not only juridically or organizationally defined forms of union, but also group formations in all the extent of their manifestation and in all the fluidity of their development.

2. Associational life led to a self-mobilization of social forces. Historical research into this trend in recent years has gathered extensive material, which leads to the following conclusion. It is in the formation of associations that the most widespread and significant form of social mobility must be identified. Associations in principle offered everyone the chance to join of his own free choice a group outside the constraints of his inherited social position.

At the basis of this trend lay a dynamic principle, namely, that ever new groups could be founded whenever people happened to agree on the fulfillment of some task, the realization of some value, the implementation of some idea or the defense of some interest.

3. The social changes produced in the 19th century had already been anticipated in the associational life of the 18th century, which drew its consequences both from the religious developments of the time and from the Enlightenment. Without this prehistory, the secular modernization of the 19th century could not have been achieved. This aspect of what associational life means becomes especially apparent by comparison with what happened in other countries. If modernization had difficulty in spreading to the margins of Europe (as in Russia), and is only now beginning (apart from one or two exceptions) to spread to the countries of the southern hemisphere, and has done so by quite different ways (ideologization), the fundamental reason for this is that these countries

lacked the aforesaid associational life, thanks to which people were already able to rise above their inherited rank and position, and so understand themselves as citizens of a different society than the one they had been born into.

Without unconditionally shaking off the traditional bonds and orders, people sought a means of support and a point of view by which they could be transcended in the associations, societies and leagues of the 18th century. Associational life as such aroused, as a whole, aspirations and expectations. From all this a verifiable hypothesis may be formulated: in our time associational life (in the broadest sense) is imperative if a modernization based on free choice is to be achieved. For an analysis of the history of associations makes it clear that the less the modernization process was promoted by associations themselves, the more it was imposed and instigated from on high with truly variable results.

4. The multiplicity and variety of associations give the impression that they each have served their own interests and goals. However, one would fail to grasp the real nature of associations if one tried to explain them simply on the basis of mere self-interests. The interests they represent are inseparably bound up with the general good. All associations, and not just the parties, end up—some more, some less—by participating in the affairs of the common interest, which they in part actively promote, in part passively transmit. In particular, even parties originate not out of the mere defense of vested interests, but out of the claim of representing the general conception of social life and social cohesion which they believe to be right. Even the associations of the 19th century founded to defend specific interests aimed everywhere at universal objectives and cannot be labeled as an "organizational reflex of particular interests."

5. Modernization is possible, because associations create attitudes, aspirations and orientations by which it may be fostered. If they did not, these would have to be determined from on high, and compulsorily implemented against the wishes of a population attached to its traditional patterns of life.

Of course, the associations were not the only agents of modernization, but the capacities of the state to be effective were powerfully bound up with their activities, and derived from their activities and demands the impetus for the state to go beyond what it could have hoped to achieve by its own intrinsic efforts.

We have referred to the modernization of society and its self-mobilization because sociological findings can throw light on the situation of the church. For it is no mere scientifically disguised piece of shadow-boxing to draw lessons from social developments for the history of the church, and so argue anew for the great help that the proclamation of the gospel derives from church associations of all kinds.

We may recall, for instance, the various impulses given by the "Catholic Movement" in Germany, in which men and women independently generated a powerful force of renewal in the church during the early decades of the 19th century. In various places Catholics banded together to form Catholic circles. An effectively irradiating practice of the faith among many Christians was the consequence. "Against the rationalistic sterility of theology, the secularizing tendencies of society and the far-reaching subordination of the church to the state, this attempt to recall reflection to the nature and history of the church wanted to establish a valid alternative."[46]

It is worth mentioning at least four of these circles.

The circle of Princess Amalia Gallitzin (d. 1806) in Münster. This circle, whose members included among others the educationalist Bernhard Overberg and Canon Franz Ferdinand von Fürstenberg, reacted against the rationalism of the Enlightenment and pursued a deepening of the faith inspired by religious sentiment.

The circle around St. Clemens Maria Hofbauer (d. 1820) in Vienna. This circle, whose members included Friedrich Schlegel and other prominent converts, combatted Josephinism and propounded a closer bond of the church with the pope.

The Landshut circle around Johann Michael Sailer (d. 1832), to which Franz von Baader and Joseph Görres also belonged. This circle promoted the rapprochement between Catholicism and modern German culture (especially intellectual). Sailer developed within it a new kind of theology based on Scripture and patristics. He had an enduring influence thanks to his numerous disciples and friends.

The circle of the seminary in Mainz. It aimed at the proper training of priests, but was of even more importance in terms of its opposition to the Enlightenment and the idea of a state church. It gave rise in 1821 to the establishment of a periodical, *Der Katholik*, which formed the foundation stone for the German Catholic press as a whole.

Roger Aubert, one of the leading experts on the history of the Catholic Church in the 19th century, maintains that all these forces initiated a "spiritual renewal . . . more consonant with history" than that of the previous reorganization of the church, as embodied for instance in the Bavarian Concordat (1817) or the bull *De Salute Animarum* (1821).

In church associations, each member of the church of every period had, and still has, the chance of being able to pursue the tasks, values, ideas and interests that seem to him important, without turning his back on the obligatory ecclesiastical order or throwing off the obligations he has assumed. Yet it is not only on account of their immediate goals that the associations constitute a source of richness in the church. That richness also flows from the readiness of their members as a whole to let the gospel transform their lives through a new willingness to listen to it, to abandon the tired routine, and shrug off fixed habits. It is by pointing to the greater mental agility acquired in this way that we can counter the argument that the members of the spiritual movements simply represent group interests. For their goals remain the goals of the gospel, and thus serve the church's mission. The spiritual movements thus make a decisive contribution to ensuring that the church is pointed in the way to greater fullness (Jn. 10:10). There are many occasions on which they can provide an impetus to authenticity and powerfully foster the church's credibility. Thanks to them, more attentive listening is devoted to the word of God, and new evangelization is made possible. Their growth in number, far from representing an obstacle to the church's mission, increases its vitality.

Just as externally the numerical growth of the groups gives a growing number of faithful the chance to find a community that responds to their situation, origin and interests, so internally, within the associations themselves, it provides the opportunity for direct communication.

Who today would want to question the high value that attaches to these opportunities? Empirical researches, artistic expressions of every kind, many observations in the course of our everyday lives and even the already mentioned problems of the sects may well convince anyone that man's yearning for community is exceeded by hardly any other need today. "It points to a change in the attitude to life, which is abandoning the hope of being able to find realization in an individual made in the image of God, and increasingly shifting to the idea that it is only as an individual in association with others and through others that a person still has the chance of developing himself."[47]

Since the very beginning, man has not lived as a self-sufficient single being, or as a cipher lost in the mass. He sees himself incorporated in the family, in the wider group and thus in a structured pattern of social relationships, which keeps him equidistant between isolation and mass disorganization. He suffers from "a very significant loss of human fullness" if he is deprived of the support of this structure. The group helps the individual to overcome disorientation and wins him over to the goals it wishes to pursue and the values it embraces. The breakdown and contraditions of man can be healed and transcended in the group. The readiness to serve, and the expectations that grow from it, are reinforced. "Man begins to become *comprehensible to himself,* and thus comprehensible to others."[48] Without objective social confirmation, man's judgment of his own capabilities and his own conceptions remains unstable and mutable. Thus the group also becomes the basis for the definition of his own values.

The above sociopsychological considerations enable us to grasp that modern man's need to communicate rightly finds a genuine response in the church's associations. At the same time, associations of every kind prove themselves to be effective centers for the formation of adults.[49] Here lies a further ground for the apostolic dynamism of renewal movements. These do not conceive of themselves as organs for the formulation of programs and strategies. These are undoubtedly necessary, but their realization is often placed in question because too few candidates present themselves for this task, and because plans on paper rarely touch the heart. Rather, they see themselves as a way of confronting the gospel and the doctrine of the church. They are open to an inner transformation, which is the authentic prerequisite for the apostolate. Indeed, this is its beginning, since the gospel, embraced in the right way, is but the mission of evangelization.

Qualified for unity

The acceptance of variety in the church—variety, above all, of forms in which the life of faith is expressed—naturally needs a reciprocal movement toward unity. Ultimate unity in the profession of faith is the supreme and irreplaceable treasure. Already the Acts of the Apostles shows the threats by which it is jeopardized. It also shows that the preservation of unity is worth every effort. Variety cannot be understood as dogmatic pluralism, as if differences or omissions should exist in the truths on which the faith and the church are founded. Anyone who minimizes or rejects the universal church's interpretation of revelation abandons himself to centrifugal movement, instead of overcoming it. He isolates and impoverishes himself. Each community of believers, whether spiritual movement or local church, needs the dual bond of unity: the "unbroken bond with the apostolic tradition of the church of the past through time" and the "bond of communion through space."[50]

The centrifugal movement indeed concerns itself more with human singularity than it does in rejoicing in the supernatural unity given to it. The consequences, for those who succumb to it in their relations with fellow believers, are self-isolation, incomprehension, rivalry, contempt and hostility. It is clear that these threats often materialize when local churches or communities of faith identify themselves with autonomous cultural areas. Theologians have pointed out that the "map of the schisms which have successively torn apart the Christian church almost completely coincides with the great cultural areas." This is so because "the sociological dynamics by which each culture is constituted normally lead it to adopt an exclusive posture,"[51] which then indelibly marks its judgments and decisons. There are those who regard corresponding cultural factors of supreme value in the realization of man. Culturally determined islands thus come to exist in the world of faith too, whether they are projections of specific life-styles (inspired for instance by ecology, by the struggle for liberation, by fixation on a social class) or bound up with particular cultures of an ethnic or geographical nature. "People then forget that each true culture, in spite of the 'sociological dynamics,' which have to be mentioned, has an open and universalizing character."[52] We have long left behind us the period of nationalism with its deification of each people's own distinct and inalienable ethnic quality and with its consequent claims on hegemony, which have so often led to wars in the past. In its stead, a new religious particularism has arisen in the church. The synod of bishops in 1969 drew the church's attention to this phenomenon. It also pointed out the need to take into consideration the sociocultural situation and its connected pastoral factors, in order to avert the danger of nationalistic excesses. Cardinal Zoungrana, archbishop of Ouagadougou, for instance, complained that "a form of nationalism is sometimes encountered that in truth is anti-Catholic. Whereas the Apostle Paul speaks of the church that is in Corinth or in Rome, etc., and that is always and everywhere the same, today there are people who, on the contrary, oppose the church of one nation to that of another region" (*op. cit.*, 63 ff.).

If we are correctly to understand and situate the contemporary trends that critically affect the Catholic Church today, we cannot afford to overlook the above analyses. The observer will recall that throughout the history of the church the Petrine ministry was in several periods the bulwark and salvation of spiritual renewal. It was also an effective counterforce to ecclesiastical regionalism and federalist ecclesiology.

Not only particular churches but also renewal movements can succumb to the temptation to pass themselves off as the totality of the church. A conviction of their own great importance, or the experience of hostile oppression by the ecclesiastical environment, may induce them to adopt an orientation of excessive introversion or even to group egoism. The history of spiritual movements has shown that a certain degree of independent life, with its inevitable isolation, is necessary if a fundamental truth is to develop or maintain its pastoral force. Yet, in embracing this apartness, these movements are threatened by a number of dangers: narcissism, fascination with power and dissension. Let us look at these threats in turn.

1. The aforementioned variety of spiritualities can induce the missionary to fall in love with the distinguishing features of his own mission. He is above all concerned that the truth of the faith should be encountered in its recipient's—i.e., his own—perspective, that his mission should be formed by his historical, epochal and personal situation, and that it should conform with nature and go beyond the objective doctrine to take in its subjective experience and appropriation. At the same time he may fail to take into account the fact that all these points of view are subordinated to "the same God who is working in all of them," to the same Spirit, who distributes different gifts to different people just as he chooses (1 Cor. 1:4-11;

Ep. 4:11-13)."[53] What releases and characterizes a spirituality is thus not the person of its founder—however indispensable he may be—but its mission from above. Otherwise, spirituality would be the product of empirically ascertainable circumstances. The origin of spirituality lies in the free choice of the Head, and aims at overflowing fullness, which has its effect in the Mystical Body. A mission thus destroys itself if it fails to recognize its source in the one Spirit, if it succumbs to narcissistic self-reflection. Only in an attitude of Marian submissiveness can it succeed.

Mary's cooperation in the history of salvation is fundamentally no other than the service that any mother renders to her child. She accepts it and brings it into the world. In so doing, she is moved not by reflection on her own motherhood, but by a simple recognition of the child's needs. All vocations and missions are thus only ecclesial and Marian if they leave behind any reflection on their own singularity and any concrete form it may take, and if they gaze with the eyes of Mary on Jesus Christ alone, in order to find in his deeds and in his will the rule for their own conduct and the answers to all their questions. It is inconceivable, for instance, to imagine a St. Francis who contemplated "Franciscanism," and not Jesus Christ alone, Jesus who in his poverty is the source of all wealth that comes from God. When it is a case of giving a shape and form to God's work in history, the founders will certainly let the laws of natural-supernatural wisdom prevail. Still, for them mission and mandate are not the end, but the means. They are not the objects of reflection and delimitation; they remain unconscious, in order to transmit the thing itself, the gospel of Jesus Christ, in ever new and ever more striking ways.

Therefore, one of the criteria for the discernment of spirits is an overt or covert devaluation of the communion of others, their suspicion or disparagement. "An antipathy nurtured within the church has never yet provided the foundation for a building up of the body of Christ (Ep. 4:12)" (*op. cit.*, 239). The discrediting of another movement or form has never yet provided the proof of one's own quality. On the contrary, the recognition of the Holy Spirit of God in the ecclesial reality of others is the proof of the powerful action of God in one's own community. What joins the great men in the history of the church together is not the different forms of their ministry, but the depths of salvific reality which they drew on, each in his own way. "The peculiarity of each of their forms is thus the antithesis of mutual delimitation. Rather, it is the means of communication itself" (*op. cit.*, 236 ff.).

2. If the consciousness that a community has of being something astounding (Ac. 8:9) comes from outside, then it may give rise to an impetus to hegemony. A reflection on spiritual movements must therefore necessarily consider the relationship between the Spirit of Christ and the use of power in the church. That orientation must be based on the conduct of Christ, who quite clearly warned about the need for prudence and caution vis-à-vis worldly influence and social power, however nobly the quest for such power might be motivated by the purpose of wielding it so as to be able effectively to evangelize and reform society. Anyone who looks at the Lord will discover other guidelines, although in the historical context of his life a step into the kingdom of this world would undoubtedly have been possible for him, indeed, even within easy reach.[54]

That Jesus Christ was conscious of his power is beyond doubt, but he always sees power as power "from above" (Jn. 19:11). Whoever adopts power in the worldly sense does not understand the sense of Jesus' mission (Mt. 20:24 ff.). Jesus speaks and teaches "as one having authority" (Mt. 7:29). He remits sins because he has "authority on earth" to do so (Mt. 9:6). He has the authority to act as supreme judge (Jn. 5:25 ff.). He has been entrusted with "authority over all people" (Jn. 17:2). Still, he repeatedly points out, and never forgets, that all this power comes to him from the Father. Even the risen and transfigured Christ declares that all the authority he has to send his disciples throughout the whole world has been given to him (Mt. 28:18).

All his power is therefore subordinated to obedience to the Father. It is inseparably bound up with his act of supreme obedience, his death on the cross, "so much so that this may take on the paradoxical form of the powerlessness of the cross, in which the power to reconcile the world takes on its full configuration" (*op. cit.*, 370).

The authority of the disciples, too, springs from the mandate they received. It cannot be severed from that source by the one who is sent. The disciple's authority is thus, like that of Christ himself, determined by obedience. The use of worldly power cannot be its goal (Mt. 10). The authority of those who follow in the footsteps of Christ is distinguished by the cross.

When that authority is removed from the disciples, it is no loss. In the early church they even experienced joy in its deprivation; the Apostles were "rejoicing that they had been judged worthy to suffer dishonor for the sake of the name" (Ac. 5:41). For the same reason, a church that is oriented toward the gospel will not—in contrast to many sects—choose propaganda as its mode of spreading the gospel. Its one concern is authentic witness. "The strongest force of publicity of the church consists in the fact that she does not publicize herself" (*op. cit.*, 374). This rule cannot be ignored by the renewal movements, and it need not diminish their certainty of the contribution their own mission makes to the present condition of the world and its political and cultural shaping.

Fascination with worldly power inevitably leads the renewal movements that succumb to it into error. The much-vaunted "realism" in relations with the forces of social influence must not lead them to aim at a revival of theocratic conceptions in their mode of re-evangelization.

3. Nor must they emancipate themselves from the sacramental structure of the church, perhaps as a result of marked hostility on the part of a local church. It is the ministry in the church, whether at the local or universal level, that is ultimately responsible for the genuineness of charisms. It is up to it to make the binding judgment, after the examination and discernment of spirits. This judgment has validity, even if it sometimes invites upon itself the blame for deaf inflexibility, as when a "charismatic spirit" disturbs its repose with necessary criticism or propounds a novelty out of joint with the times (Mary Ward and her Institute of Mary is a chastening example of this).[55]

Extreme tensions are only to be expected from renewal. They should be withstood in obedience both to the church and to God. If necessary, they should be tackled by opposition face to face (Gal. 2:11). In other words, they should not be permitted to be magnified or fomented by the interference of the public media, eager for conflict. The faith tells us that the patient support of them will be recompensed with special blessings and copious spiritual fruits.

Those responsible for the church's ministry cannot ignore the fact that forms of renewal of the church inspired and sustained by the Spirit rarely derive their initial impulse from the church herself. On her ministers is conferred the authority to guide and rule, not the authority "to root up and to tear down" claimed by Jeremiah in the Old Testament (Jer. 1:10; 31:28). In his second letter to the Corinthians (10:8; 13:10), Paul twice underlines the fact that his authority was for building up and not pulling down. Thus, the authority given to the Apostles to bind and loose can only be understood in the positive sense: binding the better to be able to loose, expulsion of the licentious from the community and his handing over to Satan "so that his spirit may be saved on the day of the Lord" (1 Cor. 5:5 ff.). "All the authority of the church's hierarchy is but the concrete mediation of Christ's way of thinking" (op. cit., 371).

NOTES

1. S. Kierkegaard, *Die Einzelne und sein Gott*, Freiburg 1961, 30-56.

2. Cited in J. Blinzler, *"Jesus und seine Junger,"* in: *Die Zeit Jesu*, ed. J. Schulz, Stuttgart 1966, 73-82, here 76.

3. J. Ratzinger, *"Zur Frage nach dem Sinn des priesterlichen Dienstes,"* in: *Geist und Leben—Zeitschrift für Aszese und Mystik*, 41 (1968), 347-376, here 355.

4. See on the following H.U. von Balthasar, *Theodramatik*, II, 2, Einsiedeln 1978, 410-424, here 412.

5. H.U. von Balthasar develops these thoughts in his *Theologik*, III, Einsiedeln 1987, 340-380, here 376.

6. See H.U. von Balthasar, *Herrlichkeit*, III, 2, 2, Einsiedeln 1969, 178.

7. P.L. Berger and T. Luckmann, *Die gesellschaftliche Konstruction der Wirklichkeit: Eine Theorie der Wissensoziologie*, Frankfurt, 4th end., 1974, 74.

8. See *inter alia* P.J. Cordes, *Sendung zum Dienst: Exegetisch-historische und systematische Studien zum Konzilsdekret "Vom Dienst und Leben der Priester*, Frankfurt 1972. The clearly defined profile of the theology of the ordained ministry in the church should in no way be underestimated by the renewal movements. Various historical episodes warn against them doing so: thus J. Wach (*op. cit*, chapter 1, note 5) describes, in his *Religionssoziologie*, the progressive schism of the Old Believers (*Starovery*) within the Russian Orthodox Church. Groups of believers at first felt revulsion for the reforms brought in by Patriarch Nikon (d. 1681) and tried to reorganize themselves to preserve their own threatened identity. Two different approaches then emerged: part of them supported the retention of fundamental doctrines, rites and institutions, but their continuation within the mainstream church was subverted by their failure to find enough ordained priests to share their ideas. The second group, by contrast, declared their definitive rupture with the Russian Orthodox Church, since they radically criticized its fundamental principles and

thus mounted a principled opposition to its ministers. According to Wach, this concrete case exemplified the fate that lies in store for those attempts at renewal that come into conflict with the representatives of the sacrament of Holy Orders. It was the rejection of the latter—whether voluntary or involuntary—by the Old Believers that turned them into a sect.

9. H.U. von Balthasar, *Theologik*, III, *op. cit.* (chapter 4, note 5), 378.

10. See *Bonhoeffer-Auswahl* (selected works), vol. 3, Munich 1970, 148. For Bonhoeffer's experiences at Finkenwalde, the underground seminary he directed from 1935 until 1940, see D. Bonhoeffer, *The Cost of Discipleship*, London 1959, 12; and *ibid.*, *The Way to Freedom. Letters, Lectures and Notes 1935-1939*, tr. E.H. Robertson and John Bowden, New York 1966, 29 ff.

11. See P.J. Cordes, *op. cit.* (chapter 4, note 8), 92-103.

12. H.U. von Balthasar, *Theodramatic*, II, 2, *op. cit.* (chapter 4, note 4), 258.

13. See G. Grundlach, articles on *"Orden,"* in: A. Vierkandt (ed.), *Handbuch der Soziologie*, Stuttgart, 2nd edn., 1961, 399-405.

14. See the progress report on "Sects or New Religious Movements: Pastoral Challenge," in *L'Osservatore Romano*, English edn., no. 20, May 19, 1986, 6.

15. H.U. von Balthasar, *Christliche Stand*, Einsiedeln 1977, 180.

16. On the following see *ibid.*, 286-294.

17. The following account is based on H.U. von Balthasar, *Herrlichkeit*, I, *op. cit.* (chapter 1, note 18), 367-380.

18. Munich 1950.

19. J.F. Six, *Itineraire spirituel de Charles de Foucault*, Paris 1958, 45.

20. *Ibid.*, note 7.

21. R. Guardini, *Die Sinne und die religiöse Erkenntnis*, Munich 1950, 55.

22. J. Pieper, *Eine Theorie des Festes*, Munich 1963, 85.

23. See *Vicesimus Quintus Annus*, the apostolic letter of John Paul II of May 13, 1989, marking the 25th anniversary of the promulgation of the *Constitution on the Sacred Liturgy* of the Second Vatican Council, here no. 7. English text in: *L'Osservatore Romano*, English edn., no. 22, May 22, 1989, 7 ff.

24. See A. Lagarde and L. Michard (eds.), *Texte et Littèrature, Xxème siècle*, Paris 1962, 177.

25. Compare the scholastic axiom *"Nihil est in intellectu, quod non prius fuerit in sensibus."*

26. A biographical account can be found in N. Glatzer, *Franz Rosensweig: His Life and Thought*, New York 1970.

27. *Ibid.*, 25. On the liturgy of Yom Kippur See *Der Talmud, Ausgewählt, übersetzt und erklärt von R. Mayer*, Munich 1980, 486 ff.

28. See G. von Rad, *Theologie des Alten Testaments*, I, Munich 1962, 254.

29. *Der Talmud, op. cit.* (chapter 4, note 27), 589.

30. See for instance the statement of the Sacred Congregation for the Liturgy and the Discipline of the Sacraments ("Notification on the celebrations in groups of the 'Neo-Catechumenals'"), in *L'Osservatore Romano* of December 24, 1988.

31. Cited as the expression of an erroneous tendency in: A. Gerhards, *"Aus der Geschichte lernen? Versuche über die Liturgie der Zukunft,"* in: *Stimmen der Zeit,* 114 (1989), 473-484, here 476.

32. "Do you believe that God is One? You are quite right. The demons believe that, and shudder" (Js. 2:19).

33. V. Seible, *"Lebensbetrachtung,"* in: *Prakitsches Lexikon der Spiritualität,* ed. Christian Schutz, Freiburg 1988, 169 ff.

34. See for example *Die Feier des Stundengebetes,* Lektionar 1, Jahresreihe 6, Freiburg 1979, 135, 139, 144, 148 et al.

35. F. Heiler, *Das Gebet: Eine religionsgeschichtliche und religionspsychologische Untersuchung,* 5th edn., Munich 1923, 476.

36. W. Nigg, *"Abbé Stock am Hinrichtungspfahl,"* in: *Heilige ohne Heiligenschein,* Olten 1978, 53.

37. The text was used in the drafting of no. 90 of the *Constitution on the Sacred Liturgy.* The importance that the renewal movements attach to the liturgy sometimes leads to the question as to the legitimacy of those "eucharistic communities" which are not simultaneously parish communities, but whose members consist exclusively of the members of church associations and movements. Significant guidelines on this problem are given by Canon Law. The relevant passages are cited by L. Gerosa, *Charisma und Recht,* Einsiedeln 1988, 272:

a) The free organization and creative form of the eucharistic celebrations in the various ecclesial associations and movements should involve no danger of in any way obscuring the fundamental structure of the sacrament of the Eucharist;

b) the said eucharistic celebrations should never leave the impression that what is involved in them is a private act of those present and not an action of the whole church and thus a public celebration (*op. cit.,* 271). On the other hand, it is equally true that the public nature of the *celebratio eucharistica* is guaranteed neither by the time nor place of the celebration, nor by the fact that it is officiated by the parish priest of those present. The *"natura publica et socialis cuisvis Missae"* (*Sacrosanctum Concilium,* 27.2) is guaranteed by the fact that it is officiated by a *"sacerdos valide ordinatus"* (Code of Canon Law, canon 900, par. 1), who in community with his bishop and *"sub eius auctoritate"* (canon 899, par. 2) conducts the community celebration in such a way that all the faithful present may derive from it *"plurimos fructus"* (canon 899, par. 3).

38. See for instance H.U. von Balthasar, *"Spiritualität,"* in: *idem, Verbum Caro: Skizzen zur Theologie,* I, Einsiedeln 1960, 226-244.

39. *Ibid., "Das Evangelium als Norm und Kritik aller Spiritualität,"* in: idem, *Spiritus Creator,* Einsiedeln 1967, 247-263, here 261.

40. H. de Lubac, *Credo: Gestalt und Lebendigkeit unseres Glaubensbekenntnisses*, Einsiedeln 1975, 204 ff.

41. St. Augustine, *De Trinitate*, lib. 15, c. 28, no. 51 (PL 42, 1098). English translation in: Saint Augustine, *The Trinity*, tr. Stephen McKenna, CSSR (*The Fathers of the Church*, vol. 45), Washington D.C. 1963, 524 ff.

42. See H.U. von Balthasar, *Spiritualität, op. cit.* (chapter 4, note 38).

43. Y. de Montecheuil, *"Verité et diversité dans l'Eglise,"* in: P. Chaillet (ed.), *L'Eglise est une: Hommage à Moehler*, Paris 1939, 252.

44. The following ideas are based on A. Hahn, *"Differenzierung, Zivilisationsprozess, Religion: Aspekte der Moderne,"* in *Kölner Zeitschrift für Sociologie und Socialpsychologie*, Sonderheft 27/1986: *"Kultur und Gesellschaft,"* ed. F. Neidhardt and M.R. Lesius, 214-231.

45. F.H. Tenbruck and W.A. Ruopp, in: *Kölner Zeitschrift für Sociologie und Socialpsychologie*, Sonderheft 25-1983: *"Gruppensociologie: Perspektiven und Materialien,"* 65-74.

46. R. Aubert, *"Anfänge der katholischen Bewegung in Deutschland und in der Schweiz,"* in *Handbuch der Kirchengeschichte*, VI, 1, 259-271, here 262.

47. H.E. Richter, in: *Evangelische Kommentare*, November, 1974, 683-686, here 683.

48. D. Claessens, *Instinkt—Psyche—Geltung*, Cologne, 2nd edn., 1970, 171.

49. Guidelines for this pastoral field, which is so important, are provided, in the form of a series of theses, by the document *The Formation of the Laity*, published by the Pontifical Council for the Laity (Vatican City 1987).

50. H. de Lubac, *Quellen Kirchlicher Einheit, op. cit.* (chapter 3, note 7), 59.

51. H.M. Legrand, *"Inverser Babel,"* in *Spiritus*, 43, 336.

52. H. de Lubac, *op. cit.* (chapter 3, note 7), 62.

53. H.U. von Balthasar, *Spiritualität, op. cit.* (chapter 4, note 38), 234.

54. M. Hengel, *Gewalt und Gewaltlosigkeit: Zur "politischen Theologie" in neutestamentlichen Zeit*, Stuttgart 1971. See on the following H.U. von Balthasar, *Theologik*, III, *op. cit.* (chapter 4, note 5), 369-375.

55. The English 17th-century lay apostle Mary Ward wanted to found an order of uncloistered nuns without any distinctive habit. Her ideas were regarded as dangerously novel, and their Ignatian spirit aroused opposition. The growth of her institute brought more attacks, and eventually led (in 1629) to its suppression. Mary herself was considered a rebel. She was confined for a short time in a convent in Munich, released after a personal appeal to the pope, and returned to England, where she died in 1646. It was only in 1877 that Mary Ward's institute received final papal approval. Pius XII (1951) praised her as *"cette femme incomparable,"* and ranked her with St. Vincent de Paul as promoter of the lay apostolate.

V. A tribute to
Hans Urs von Balthasar[1]

The present book would not have been conceivable without Hans Urs von Balthasar's alertness to the signs of the times, or without his extraordinary spiritual and intellectual vigor. This is shown not only by the many bibliographical references to his writings to be found in these pages, but also by a more pervasive presence. It is therefore only right and proper that his life and work should be more explicitly recalled at the end of this book, not least because the starting point of his work is formed by what constitutes the decisive feature of the new evangelization, namely, that man and his world are irrevocably ordained to God.

Søren Kierkegaard, whom Balthasar held in high regard, bitterly lamented the fact that large auditoriums and the applause of the masses lead to untruth. It is only in the individual that our true nature is clearly revealed (see above, chapter 4.1). Now, Balthasar showed his friendliness and affection for man to the individual. I think of his letters, in which he gave scrupulous and precise answers to questions, drafted rapidly in his beautiful handwriting. I recall a visit I made to his house in Basel in February, 1982, when he made half a day free for me, since I had a number of questions to put to him and needed his advice. Nor did he forget, on that occasion, to point out the Kunstmuseum in Basel to me and recommend that I should visit it. I remember, also, an afternoon in Rome, when I happened to be visiting our San Lorenzo International Youth Center and found him praying alone in the dark Romanesque church. I remember, too, an evening meal we had together, when we were both invited as guests by Don Giussani[2] at *Le Cappellette*. I was impressed on that occasion by his amazing knowledge of classical music. He knew by heart all the great symphonies and concertos for solo instruments, but he then confided that he had given away all his disks, so as to find more time for his theological work. Lastly, I remember a meeting with him at Lugano in early June, 1988, after he had been made a cardinal. We spoke at table of the public reactions to his nomination. Smiling, he quoted the German Cardinal Hermann Volk's remark: "If so many are glad about it, I too must be glad."

Yet it is not only on account of his upright and winning humanity that today we remember the name of this man, however decisive these qualities may be in deciding on a man's greatness. Rather, we wish to remember him for his immeasurable spiritual and intellectual force, which induced another great man of our time, Henri de Lubac, to call him "perhaps the most cultivated man of our time."[3] De Lubac was one of his teachers; he ought to have known.

On his extensive journey through the world of the Spirit, Balthasar was impelled neither by the intellectual curiosity of the researcher nor the fame bestowed on the pundit. First and foremost Balthasar was a pastor of souls. It is symptomatic that, after the completion of his Jesuit education, he should have decided not to pursue a university career. At the age of 30 he had ended his training in the Society of Jesus. His superior offered him the choice of either opting for a chair of dogmatics or being appointed chaplain of the student community in Basel. He chose service as a priest. Even when he later came to discuss the main priorities of his activity, it was the spiritual and pastoral sphere that unquestionably came first on the list. In the account of himself he gave in his 60s, he put the number of retreats he had given around a hundred[4]—and he wasn't talking about some weekend retreats, but the classical Spiritual Exercises of St. Ignatius. Besides, one has only to read a bit of his very personal account called *Unser Auftrag (Our Task)*[5] to perceive the fundamental impulse of this man, namely, the wrestling with man to achieve his submission to a God greater than he, as in the comments of Adrienne von Speyer on his Exercises, and also in the plan and goals of the *Johannes Gemeinschaft* (Community of St. John).

It was, in brief, his concern for man and for his salvation that was the driving force of his life. At first he wanted to orientate the Christian life by the pursuit of direct pastoral guidance to others and personal priestly service. Then he took on the task of reviewing and elucidating anew the entire heritage of the spiritual history of the West: philosophy from the pre-Socratics to Heidegger, the theological treasures of patristics, through the great Doctors of the church, down to the historical and critical exegesis of Karl Barth. Balthasar also occupied himself with the empirical human sciences of the present day and, at an advanced age, confessed that the great modern novels exercised so strong a fascination over him that he had not yet been able to conquer the vice of devouring them. "He could never be accused of scorning what he didn't know," de Lubac affirms,[6] undoubtedly an unusual quality in an age in which the mountain of human knowledge is growing ever more dauntingly, and the great mass of mankind either skirts it thanks to unshakable prejudice or ascends it in the cable car of journalistic superficiality. Balthasar, on the other hand, drew up his own plan to expose that mountain once again to the light of revelation, for man's sake.

For the sake of man who, from the Renaissance onward, had progressively become detached from the cosmos, to the point that he can no longer understand himself as a being among others. With the loss of his consciousness of his having been created, and of forming part of a living creation, man has been deprived at the same time of the security and protection that his createdness vouchsafes. Instead of being safely housed in the creation, all he was left with was a feeling of vulnerability. Only one thing can deliver him from the crisis of his sense of abandonment: he must once again find his security in God.

Henri de Lubac explained Balthasar's analysis of man as follows. In our time man's relationship with God acquires "a heightened urgency; the biblical doctrine of man being created in the image of God acquires a sharper profile, and, without any need to jettison the stages of natural knowledge, the revelation of Jesus Christ is presented to him as the necessary answer to the question posed by his whole being. Jesus in his temporal and historical existence . . . leads man to the revelation of the unknown being that he himself was" (*op. cit.*, 394). In other words, God offers the outcast man a place in Jesus Christ and the image of Jesus for his own self-understanding.

To make man aware of God's presence in Jesus Christ means conducting a theological enterprise worthy of its name. According to Balthasar, the heritage of the Western spirit can be arranged in three thematic circles.[7] "Theo-aesthetic" is the first heading under which he subsumes his systematic overview; here *"aisthesis,"* it should be underlined, means not the "doctrine of beauty," but should be understood in its more original sense of the perception (and hence acknowledgement) of the created and what is re-created in Christ, while *"aistheton"* means what has thus been perceived (and acknowledged), which is self-radiating love. Balthasar's work in question—in German *Herrlichkeit*, i.e., splendor, magnificence, glory—remains at the level of light, image and appearance. That is only one dimension of the knowledge of God. The next dimension is called "deed and event." This is how Balthasar conceives the "Theo-dramatic": God who acts in man. Man responds through decision and deeds. Mission is here established definitively as the central concept of Christology and the imitation of Christ. This is followed, lastly, by what Balthasar called "Theo-logic," i.e., the exposition of what is meant by "truth" in the event of the revelation of God through the incarnation of the *Logos* and the pouring out of the Spirit; of the relationship of the structure of the creation to divine truth; and how, in the aftermath of revelation, human testimony can credibly bear witness to the truth of God.

In 1965 Balthasar was still afraid he would be unable to bring his vast undertaking to completion. Others, he wrote, would have to continue the dialogue with the great figures of the past. In effect, in the development of the *magnum opus* itself one can detect signs of growing haste, forced on him by the inexorable passage of time. Indeed, he laments the fact that he had been obliged "to bundle together into a miserable paragraph" themes which would have demanded a whole book.[8] Yet he did in fact succeed in completing the work—this 12-volume *summa*, each volume running to some 600 pages— which leaves the reader truly breathtaken and awed.

The theocentric titles of the plan of the work speak an unequivocal language. Human aesthetic, action and logic can only receive their light from God. Moreover, Balthasar wanted, in enunciating these three categories, to place God and his work at the center of human thought. He does so at a time when thought seems to be inebriated by cosmic euphoria; a time when what should rather be called anthropology is passed off as the science of God. Balthasar places his theocentrically dictated plan in contraposition to the many attempts that come under the title of theology, but ought to be distinguished as downright philosophy: the various "theologies of earthly realities," "of labor," "of development," "of the ethical situation."[9]

The pastor of souls in Balthasar perceives the damage

caused to man by these purported works of theology, and reacts resolutely against them. At times he is possessed by the indignation of St. Paul. It was not the theoretical curiosity of the researcher that impelled him, but an insight into the threats posed to human salvation. No one can expect dispassionate objectivity from such a conviction. Prophetic appeals are in the last analysis born from a state of emergency, from the actual threat impending over man. The threat, for instance, posed by the erosion of divine truth by rationalism.[10] Balthasar saw that the "battle of the *Logos*" was taking place, since reason was increasingly dissolving the mysteries of God. Reason is pressing forward "into the divine grounds" of existence and leading to the God of Hegel, the God shorn of mystery, and to the "doors of atheism." The wish to explain everything has, according to Balthasar, not only shaken, but subverted the foundations of Christian thought. The articles of faith are no longer the hidden object of Christian theologizing, but they themselves, by a strange reversal of understanding, are subjected to rational inquiry with the goal of formulating them anew, and pruning their content to make it plausible to a secularized, nontranscendental view of the world. If the church's authority should persist in pretending that the contents of the faith bequeathed to her *ab antiquo* are still binding, then she too is subjected to a critical inquiry, and asked to provide proofs of her authority.

Rationalism, according to Balthasar, has penetrated theology as a new form of gnosis, and demands more categorically than ever its rightful place in it. It claims to be the criterion for an effective *aggiornamento* and the precondition for the evangelization of the contemporary world. Moreover, it is claimed to provide the common basis on which a rapprochement with nonbelievers can be sought, and their understanding of what it means to be a Christian achieved (*op. cit.*, 249).

Balthasar thus regards resistance as inevitable even within the church. His analysis is apocalyptically pointed: "This anthropocentric, unbelieving enlightenment increasingly has at its disposal ever more effective means of influencing the masses, and of forcing into the defensive, and even into the minority, all those who fight for the integralness of the faith. The saying of Jesus, that the disciples were being sent out like sheep among wolves (Mt. 10:16), is thus gaining in vividness" (431 ff.).

The lamentation, perhaps, of an old and disappointed man? Hardly. To endorse Balthasar's view, it is enough to think of the recent antipapal invectives of certain university professors and of the chorus of approbation they met with in almost all the media. The role of the pastor in Balthasar, moreover, cautions us against the too rash disqualification of his warnings, as if they could be conveniently written off under the rubric of frustration and polemics. Again and again his avowals of a God who is stronger than we are give hope to the despised and rejected in the contemporary context. In one of his long essays—one of the series of papers and books that he published alongside his *magnum opus*—Balthasar makes it quite clear that, if his diagnosis is negative, this is solely motivated by the desire to find a cure.

Yet Balthasar's thought cannot be totally comprehended by his theocentrism alone, however determined and mystically profound this was. If it is regarded in isolation, it could raise the suspicion that what he was recommending was flight from the world, or extreme other-worldliness. His proclamation of the absoluteness of God never raises with it the suspicion that he was propagating spiritual self-sufficiency or endorsing the egoistic enjoyment of individual piety. For in fact he never tires of realistically affirming that the hour of truth for our Christian lives comes in our dealings with our fellow men. It is not enough to speak with the tongues of men and of angels, to understand all mysteries and all knowledge, to remove mountains by faith, and give up the body to be burned. Without love, all this serves nothing (1 Cor. 13:1 ff.). "Only love is credible."[11]

How can man succeed in loving his fellow men? Even his enemy? Balthasar has no illusions. Man alone, man unaided, is incapable of loving. In his encounter with his fellow men he dies of asphyxia. If I only find in the other person what I know in the depths of my own being—the limitations of my own nature, anxieties about what it is that marks my confines: death, disease, madness, adversity—why should my "I" lose itself in a "you" whom, in the last analysis, I can only see as myself? "No, if I do not encounter God in my own kind, if love does not imbue me with a breath of the presentiment of eternity, if I cannot love my neighbor with a love that comes from much farther away than my own finite capacity to love, and if what in our relationship bears the sublime name of love does not come from God or lead back to him, then the enterprise is not worth a candle. It would liberate man neither from his self-imprisonment nor from his solitude."[12]

It should be no cause for surprise, therefore, that Balthasar, so disturbed as he was by the climate of godlessness in our time, should constantly urge and seek to obtain the turning toward God. He does this especially by reiterating that all service to the gospel and to the mission of the church can only succeed if it has its roots in prayer. This catechesis he expounds, for instance, in his book *Das betrachtende Gebet* (*The Prayer of Contemplation*), which has rightly been called "a comprehensive exposition of the Christian mystery, no more substantial than which can be found" (Henri de Lubac). Just one page of this book may exemplify the enduring actuality of Balthasar's teaching:

"Everything we can give witness to our fellow men about the reality of God derives from contemplation: of Jesus Christ, the church, ourselves. Yet no one can enduringly and effectively preach the contemplation of Jesus Christ and the church unless he himself partakes of it. Just as no one can meaningfully treat of love unless he himself has loved, or speak of even the smallest problem of the spiritual world unless he himself has had an authentic experience of it, so a Christian can only act in an apostolic way if, like the rock of Peter, he proclaims what he has seen and heard. 'We did not follow cleverly devised myths when we made known to you the power and coming of our Lord Jesus Christ, but we had been eyewitnesses of his majesty. For he received honor and glory from God the Father. . . . We ourselves heard this voice come from heaven while we were with him on the holy mountain' (2 Pt. 1:16-19)."[13]

Balthasar then continues, not without melancholy: "But who today, in all the 'dossiers' of Catholic activism, speaks of Tabor? Of seeing, hearing and touching what cannot be proclaimed and propagated unless it has previously been experienced and known? Of the inexpressible peace of eternity transcending all worldly strife, but also the unutterable frailty and helplessness of the crucified Love, from whose 'emptying' to the point of 'nothing,' to the point of 'becoming sin' and 'becoming malediction,' all the strength and salvation of the church and of mankind grows. For anyone who has not experienced this in contemplation, all speech about it, and even action in consequence of it, remains affected by a kind of embarrassment and bad conscience, unless this bad conscience, too, has been buried below the naivete of a kind of activism that is basically secular, and only called spiritual by a misconception."

NOTES

1. This is the text of a lecture I gave to the Meeting for Friendship among Peoples, in 1989 at Rimimi, Italy.

2. Luigi Giussani founded the Communion and Liberation movement in 1953.

3. H. de Lubac, "*Eine Zeuge Christi in der Kirche: Hans Urs von Balthasar,*" in: *Internationale Katholische Zeitschrift*, 4 (1975), 390-409, here 392.

4. *Rechenschaft 1965*, Einsiedeln 1965, 8.

5. Einsiedeln 1984, *passim*.

6. H. de Lubac, *op. cit.* (chapter 5, note 2), 33.

7. See *Rechenschaft, op. cit.* (note 3), 33.

8. *Theologik*, III, *op. cit.* (chapter 4, note 5), Foreword.

9. See *Rechenschaft, op. cit.* (chapter 5, note 3), 11.

10. See *Theodramatik*, III, *op. cit.* (chapter 1, note 3), 427-438.

11. This is the title of Balthasar's key work: *Glaubhaft ist nur Liebe*, Einsiedeln 1963.

12. H. de Lubac, *op. cit.* (chapter 5, note 2), 403.

13. *Das betrachtende Gebet*, Einsiedeln 1955, 97.

More books from Greenlawn Press

Open the Windows:
The Popes and Charismatic Renewal
Edited with an introduction by Fr. Kilian McDonnell, O.S.B.
Open the Windows is the first book to gather in English translation all
the major statements and documents of Popes Paul VI and John Paul II
on the Catholic charismatic renewal. This valuable collection shows
you how the popes have welcomed and pastored this movement. Along
with a stimulating essay on the role of baptism in the Spirit in Christian
initiation, the book gives helpful introductions to each document.

$5.95, paper, 94 pp.

Resist the Devil:
A Pastoral Guide to Deliverance Prayer
By Rev. Charles W. Harris, C.S.C.
This powerful book shows you methods of deliverance prayer and
discernment that are spiritually and psychologically sound. Fr. Harris,
an authorized diocesan exorcist, enlightens you with case histories of
real and imagined evil spiritual influences.

$6.95, paper, 118 pp.

Fishers of Men:
The Second Worldwide Retreat for Priests
Edited by Fr. Tom Forrest, C.Ss.R.
Standing in the shadow of the year 2000, no mandate looms larger than
that of worldwide evangelization. To that end, Pope John Paul II
invited 5,000 priests from around the world to the Second Worldwide
Retreat for Priests. There is much of great value for Catholics as we
are ushered into the full spirit of this retreat. Includes talks given by
Pope John Paul II and Mother Teresa.

$10.95, paper, 217 pp.

Order these books today from your local Christian bookstore or directly from:
> Greenlawn Press
> Dept. PC
> 107 S. Greenlawn Ave.
> South Bend, IN 46617

Payment must accompany order. Please add 7% for shipping and handling
(**$2.00 minimum**). Payment may be by check, money order, Visa or
Mastercard. If paying by credit card, please include on your order your credit
card number, your name as it appears on the card, the expiration date of your
card, your phone number and your signature.

You can also order by phone using your Visa or MasterCard. Phone 800-234-
5088 between 9:00 AM and 4:30 PM EST, Monday through Friday. To fax
your order dial (219) 236-6633 anytime.